SONG TITLE SERIES

PRESENTS

BON JOVI

JOAN MAGUIRE

WANTED

DEAD OR ALIVE

THE BON JOVI BAND

For being the best band ever to record and perform so many great songs over the years, whether it be live performances, in concerts recorded on video or DVD or on a CD. Keep up the good work and keep delivering great songs and performances either live or on DVD or CD

Copyright Page

New: Bon Jovi

Author: Joan Maguire

National Library of Australia Cataloguing-in-Publication – Publication entry

Author:	Maguire, Joan.
Title:	Bon Jovi/ Joan Maguire.
ISBN:	9780980855104
Series:	Song title series.
Subjects:	Bon Jovi, Jon
	Bon Jovi (Musical group)
	Rock musicians—United States--Biography
	Rock groups—United States--Biography
Dewey Number:	781.66092

Originally published with the assistance of Love of Books and is available through the Print on Demand network and www.songtitleseries.com

This short story book was created and written
By Joan Maguire on 24th July 2010 ©
ISBN: 978-0-9808551-0-4

E-book re-written April 2014© and is available through the providers
listed on www.songtitleseries.com
EIBSN: 978-0-9808551-7-3

The large print book was created in March 2015 © is available
through the same distributors as the normal book and
www.songtitleseries.com
ISBN: 978-0-9941998-6-7 (large print)

DEDICATION

I would like to dedicate and say a big THANK YOU to the guys who make up the greatest band, BON JOVI who are Jon Bon Jovi, Richie Sambora, David Bryan, Tico Torrens and Hugh McDonald (and Alec John Such). Without the well written songs, perseverance and the personal sacrifices that you have all made for your ever loyal fans; this book could not have been written.

And to say thank you to my Earth Angel David and his friends, who inspire and motivate me to achieve things that I never dreamt were possible.

INTRODUCTION

Legally I cannot use Lyrics or Music because of Copyright but I can use song titles but don't forget that because of using the original song titles (Italicized) in whole, there are places in the book that could be changed to make it more comprehensible Also due to the nature of my books; legally I must place a Reference either after each story or before the Bibliography in the back of the book.

Every song title from every album, concert on video or DVD, whether it be by the band collectively or solo pieces from each individual band member that I own, has been used in this story. It doesn't matter how many times a song has been played at different times; the title is used that many times and not just once.

Many of the pictures used in the different sections of the book were sighted on a few different internet sites; however I have only acknowledged one site in the bibliography. I have not attempted to plagiarize or to disregard anyone's copyright by the use of the pictures and the actual pictures used in this book were legally obtained at the time by the original publisher of this book.

When reading this "Song Title Series" book, I hope that no disservice has been done to the band as well as their adoring fans who read it, for that was not my intention. As I may have missed a song, an album or a concert within this book I do apologize sincerely. I have created and written this story without the sanctity of the band and I hope that if they read it, they will enjoy it as well.

Grab a drink, sit down and join Oprah as she chooses the *Big Green Freak* to tell his story of the dream he had the previous night. Follow his story through the vivid *Hollywood Dreams* and how his life today has changed from those experiences. Find out the real answer to the mysterious question that is being asked of him throughout the book and know that a total of 1,284 song titles have been used to make this story possible.

ACKNOWLEDGEMENTS

I would like to thank my daughters, Jenny and Kylie for their positive but critical input in the first draft of this book and all the help and support that they have given me throughout the Song Title Series books. With taking their input to mind, I have improved the book.

I would also like to thank my son Peter and his family for their support and help in keeping me grounded.

I would like to thank Kay and Julie for their patience and understanding whilst teaching me and giving me the skills to present my unique books in the best way possible.

I would like to thank Marcie for her help with the Spanish translation.

I would like thank everyone else who has helped me bring this book to life and to you for purchasing it.

CONTENTS

INTO THE NETHERWORLD

During the taping of one of her shows, Oprah asked if anyone had recently had any strange dreams.

"Choose me, Oprah!" said the *Big Green Freak* and I will tell you all about it.

"Go ahead and tell us what your dream was all about." Oprah said.

"Well" said the Freak, "wandering *into the Netherworld* was like wandering into many *Hollywood dreams* that you can walk through anytime you wanted to.

The time that I accidentally stumbled into it, was *August 7, 4.15* am and it was that hot; *99 in the shade* and it wasn't even the *summertime*. I was fascinated by the *endless horizon* from where many walking paths, roads and *cruising lines* would go.

On one line there was a *mystery train* that was going to a *destination anywhere*. A group of people walked around a *bed of roses* towards the train. A *colored woman* came up to me and introduced herself and said her name was *April* and *everyday* she would board the train and *have a nice day* at wherever she went and suggested that I should take a trip on the train, maybe even on the one that was leaving soon.

Curiosity welled up in me, so I boarded the train and just after we left the station, the rail staff began serving refreshments but I was warned that they *always* serve *Bitter Wine* that tasted like really *bad medicine*.

Captain Crash and the Beauty Queen from Mars were amongst the passengers in my carriage and when the music came across the speakers in the carriage they got up and did the *Netherworld Waltz* down the narrow aisle.

The train stopped to take on more refreshments at a little hut on the side of the track and during the *interlude* I looked out of the window and watched the sun set in a *blaze of glory*.

A single thought came into my head at that moment and that was *"Hey God, I believe* that *it's my life* to live the way I want to, however, I thank you for the entire world and all of its beauty. I will *keep the faith* I have in you because you do *open your heart* to everyone including those people who are *livin' in sin."*

2

I had been sitting down for quite awhile so I decided to stretch my legs and explore the rest of the train. The next carriage was fitted out like a saloon. It had a bar where you buy drinks, tables and seats, a book shelf holding many different types of books and opposite it, a notice board.

On the board was a wanted poster, not a *Wanted Dead Or Alive* poster, just a wanted poster of a *runaway* who had stolen many items including a *diamond ring*. There wasn't a reward offered, just a phone number to contact if she was sighted.

I brought myself a soft drink and while sitting at one of the tables I glanced through some of the books before heading back to my seat in the other carriage.

It seemed like we had been travelling for hours before an announcement came through the speakers in the train stating that we were approaching the first stop and if everyone could please return to their allocated seats.

As I sat down, the *runaway* approached me and asked in a quiet voice "Can I sit in the *seat next to you* until we reach the first stop because my seat is way up front in the first carriage."

I agreed.

The *runaway* continued "*Someday I'll be Saturday night* but until then *it's my life* and *everyday* I will live it as I want to for *I'll sleep when I'm dead. These days; who says you can't go home* and with *a little help from my friends,* I will make it and I hope that never in a million years, will *you give love a bad name* to anyone."

I think that I might do what that woman, April suggested and check out our first stop, even though they hadn't told us where it was.

The train pulled to a stop at the empty platform and before some of us were able to get off the train, I heard someone asks "*WHO WILL SAVE NEW JERSEY?*"

3

THE WESTERN DREAM

I had noticed that as the train approached the first destination, the countryside had changed from lush green grass and trees to a *dry county* where the grass and shrubs withered *out in the heat.* The train's first destination, *Guano City* was a *little city,* like a picture you would see on a *postcard from the Wasteland.*

Some passengers like the *runaway* alighted from the train; however *Captain Crash and the Beauty Queen from Mars* stayed on board. They were heading to a place further down the tracks because they said that *dyin' ain't much of a livin'* and that most of the citizens in that town were *all talk, no action.*

I wondered what they meant by that comment?

Once off the train, you couldn't help noticing all the signs stuck in the ground. One sign was in Spanish that read "ALEJATE DE LA *CAMA DE ROSAS.*" the other was translated into English and read "KEEP AWAY FROM THE *BED OF ROSES.*"

Someone commented that they had been there before and that in this city it seemed that *good guys don't always wear white* as some of them ended up on the *right side of wrong. These days* the city has just become a *two story town* and is *open all night* and then they got back on the train.

I found a small hotel and went in for a drink and something to eat.

The *outlaws of love* rode into town that evening *on a full moon* to have *one wild night* and they were *wild in the streets.* The citizens hoped that *maybe tomorrow* they would leave. The next morning the sun rose in a *blaze of glory* but the outlaws were still in town even though there were many *Wanted Dead Or Alive* posters of them hanging everywhere. There was also another poster of the *runaway* hanging on the wall stating that she was a *thief of hearts.*

Someone said "A terrible fight broke out at *midnight in Chelsea,* a suburb on the outskirts of town where the *bitch/slut/liar/whore* lived. I could hear people shouting "Don't you *lay your hands on me* and *you give love a bad name.* You are *always in and out of love* and you *always* think that *I'll be there for you. It's my life* and *someday I'll be Saturday night.* If you think that *in these arms* you will go out in a *blaze of glory* .... Think again."

Then somebody else shouted "*Billy get your guns* while the rest of us go into the *Church of Desire* to *say a prayer* for all the innocent people caught up in the fight." and I followed them in.

"*Hey God,* give us *something to believe in* because the trouble in this town is *starting all over again*. I don't want to see all that *blood on blood* anymore or anymore *Wanted Dead Or Alive* posters hanging up. I don't want us to keep living our lives like we're *livin' on a prayer*. I have done my best to *keep the faith* and with a *little bit of soul* and *with a little help from my friends,* I want to *breakout* of this city and *runaway* from here. Please God *hear our prayer*."

Other citizens in the church said "Lord *lay your hands on me* and help me *keep the faith* for I'm *livin' on a prayer*. Yes, please help us all to *keep the faith* for we are all *livin' on a prayer*."

Then the citizens inside the church and I heard someone outside yell "*Raise your hands*. I said *Raise your hands*." and then "*Ride cowboy ride*."

A shot was heard followed by a scream and then there was a thought of another *Wanted Dead Or Alive* poster being hung on the wall in town.

Just about everybody inside the church, including myself, rushed outside onto the church lawns and heard a man say "*I'll sleep when I'm dead* and not before but when you are *in these arms,* don't *you give love a bad name*. I also don't need any more *bad medicine* from you either."

To whom he was talking to is beyond me as I didn't see anyone else around except for the church goers behind me.

We suddenly heard somebody *shout* out that there was a *jailbreak* and everybody started running *wild in the streets*. I thought it might be best for me to find some cover as well, so instead of going back into the church I went into the *BAD MEDICINE* saloon, where I noticed that on the shelves were bottles of *BAD MEDICINE* whiskey, *BAD MEDICINE* rum and *BAD MEDICINE* wine. The bar was covered with *Wanted Dead Or Alive* posters that were varnished. They seemed very appropriate for this bar in this town.

About ten minutes after the people had settled in the saloon, a couple of men from the *breakout* ran through a *bed of roses* outside the front door, through the saloon and out the back door.

5

As the Deputies followed the escapees through the saloon, it seemed that there was a *whole lot of leaving* by the other patrons trying to get out of there quickly incase there was a gun fight.

During the commotion, the *runaway* disappeared upstairs with another one of the escapees and I heard him say to her as they were going up "You were *born to be my baby* and never do *you give love a bad name*. In fact *I'd die for you* so while we can, won't you *lay your hands on me* for *someday I'll be Saturday night*."

"*I'll be there for you* and I will be there for you *everyday*. We must both *keep the faith* and not to be *livin' on a prayer*." said the *runaway* as they were standing at the top of the stairs.

Another *shout* was heard, telling the Deputies about the man upstairs and they came rushing through the front door. The escapee who was upstairs jumped through a window into a *bed of roses* and then climbed onto a horse and rode off as the *runaway* said in a low voice "*Ride cowboy ride*."

The Deputies questioned the *runaway* to find out where the escapee would go but all she would say to them was "What escapee? I'm here by myself so please leave and *have a nice day*."

People were still going *wild in the streets* and there was an awful lot of *blood on blood* everywhere. Eight men broke out of jail and all of them were *wanted dead or alive*. Two of them tried to go out in a *blaze of glory* but were shot in the back while trying to get away, leaving more *blood on blood* on the ground.

Another escapee who was held up in the corner store fired his gun at the Sheriff but all the bullet did was *bounce* of the wall.

Then he yelled "I may be *wanted dead or alive* but *it's my life* and I may be *livin' on a prayer* but I will *keep the faith* and hope that I will go out in a *blaze of glory*. *Someday I'll be Saturday night* and *I'll sleep when I'm dead*."

The Sheriff took aim with his rifle and said "Did you say *I'll sleep when I'm dead*. Well if you did, then sleep well." and fired, killing the man.

An innocent man was cornered near the bakery and the Deputies said "*Raise your hands*."

6

The man replied "I'm not *wanted dead or alive* so don't *lay your hands on me; it's my life* you're threatening here. If you look closely, you will see that I am *just older* than the men you are looking for. *These days* it's so easy to be mistaken for somebody else."

The Deputies apologized and said that they *misunderstood* what was being yelled at them and told him to *have a nice day* before they went on their way.

Above the saloon, the saloon owner's daughter was heard crying and upon investigation by the Sheriff, another escapee was captured. The Sheriff said "*Raise your hands* and don't try to run. You are *livin' on a prayer* as it is."

The escapee turned as he was being led away and said to the young woman "*I'd die for you* if you had been *born to be my baby*. You know *you give love a bad name* and when you *lay your hands on me* I get a bad *fever* and if I don't *keep the faith* I have then I know that I will be *damned*."

The Sheriff and his Deputies were *undivided* in their attempts to recapture or kill all the escapees.

The Sheriff stated that all the escapees who were still at large were *livin' on a prayer* and that they won't last long on the run once we re-issue *Wanted Dead Or Alive* posters with a larger amount of *blood money* as a reward.

One of the Deputies then said "*Who says you can't go home* as that is where the escapees might be heading. Their mothers might tell them "You have been *misunderstood* and never will *you give love a bad name* for *I'll be there for you always* if you need me because you were *born to be my baby*."

Then another *shout* was heard and the Sheriff turned and stood face to face with the meanest man who was *wanted dead or alive*. They both drew their guns and fired but the Sheriff was the *last man standing*.

That was *the last night* that I intended to stay in that town and everybody started drinking that wine stuff; the one that tasted like really *bad medicine* that I didn't like, just to calm down after the commotion during that day.

I thought "Had the *radio saved my life tonight?*

I don't think so because they weren't around in those days. *It's my life* and *everyday* I have to make choices and *who says you can't go home* if you want to. But for me to go home, I would have had to get out of this town."

The following morning there was already a *whole lot of leaving* going on and people were trampling through the *bed of roses* to get on the bus that travelled down the *Lost Highway* because the train was no longer there nor was the station.

As we left the town I heard someone in the distance ask "WHO WILL SAVE NEW JERSEY?"

THE GANGSTER DREAM

Finally I was right away from that awful town. *It's a long road* this *Lost Highway* and we're still travelling through the same *dry county,* where there's no green grass or trees to be seen and there aren't many farms of any sort either.

There were so many *Wanted Dead Or Alive* posters posted all around that last city that I don't know how the citizens could live there. Maybe it's because they did *keep the faith* and believed that they are not *livin' on a prayer.*

I hoped the next place we were going to stop at was better, wherever it was and *come Saturday night,* tomorrow night, we would be there and I would find out.

After two days of travelling on that bus, we finally arrived in *Santa Fe.* I thought that this looked like another place where *good guys don't always wear white.* At least there weren't any *Wanted Dead Or Alive* posters, posted all over the buildings walls.

The hotel where we were staying in, was owned and run by *Brother Louie,* an old gangster, who would talk to you pleasantly; but *don't you believe him* as he would soon *bounce* you out of the door if you disagreed with him or he would baffle you by *stringin' a line* about how good the *everyday* life and people were in that town.

The hotel had a Dining and Entertainment Room where you could eat, listen to the band or dance to the *Netherworld Waltz.* It had a Gaming Room where you could play the slot machines, *roulette* or poker.

In the Entertainment Room I noticed that the bar had *Wanted Dead Or Alive* posters stuck all along it under the varnish and behind the bar on shelves, the same drinks as in the last town were for sale, *BAD MEDICINE* whiskey, *BAD MEDICINE* rum and *BAD MEDICINE* wine.

I asked the bar attendant where it came from and he said "We have *always* carried the stock but I think the Indians named it because alcohol was *bad medicine* for them as it made them do crazy things. After drinking it they went *wild in the streets* and seemed to fight all the time, leaving *blood on blood* everywhere. They would tell everyone they met *"You give love a bad name"* then a few days later they would disappear into the *dry county* to sober up."

There was a band playing *Rockin' all over the World* when I entered the Entertainment room and now they're singing *Como Yo Nadie Te Ha Arma*. I asked the bar attendant when I went to get another drink about the song and he said "translated it means *This Ain't a Love Song*."

Coming from another room, I heard Louie say "*Janie, don't take your love to town* because I will *always* love you and *I'll be there for you. We rule the night* together but you know that I'm *lonely at the top* and you know that you were *born to be my baby*. You know that *I'd die for you*. Babe, *this ain't a love song* and remember that *dyin' ain't much of a livin'*."

Janie replied by saying "*These days* we get *more than we bargained for*. I know that you say you love me, that you will lay me on a *bed of roses* where you will *lay your hands on me* and give me a *diamond ring* but I don't love you because *you give love a bad name*. You are *always in and out of love* with me and other women. *It's my life* and *someday I'll be Saturday night* and I won't have to be *livin' on a prayer* anymore."

As she turned and walked away through the Entertainment room she said "You are nothing but a *hound dog*. You *always lie to me* so *hearts breaking even* tonight is the best deal I can offer; otherwise I will *live fast, love hard, die young. Everyday* you *shout* at me and say *you give love a bad name* but you never say *have a nice day*."

Louie said "I only *shout* because you turn your hearing aides off and it's the only way I can be heard." and he started to follow her, pulling out a small gun from his belt as he did.

Janie thought "*It's my life* and it's the only way I can get a *silent night. I don't like Mondays* but *I don't want to fall to the fire* of a *bullet* either and that's what I'll get if I stay here much longer."

Louie thought "*This woman is dangerous* and the *justice in the barrel* of this gun will be a *shot through the heart*."

As he fired the gun, he knew that he had missed her and had hit a band member. He went over to the guitarist who was slumped against a large amplifier covered in blood and said surprisingly "*Why aren't you dead*. I thought you would be?"

The guitarist replied "Because *my guitar lies bleeding in my arms* as it took most of the impact of the bullet.

10

With all this *blood on blood* would you please call an ambulance because *it's my life* that is hanging in the balance here and they will give me *something for the pain*. I have no intentions of going out in a *blaze of glory* however if I do die, please bury me under a *cama de rosa (bed of roses)*.

Hey God, don't let my guitar die *in these arms*. I know that *I'll sleep when I'm dead* because I am not *livin' on a prayer* and I will *keep the faith* I have in you so I will never be *damned.*"

Then he passed out.

When the shot was fired, there was a *shout* of "Get down and get out." and then there was a *whole lot of leaving* from the patrons in the Entertainment Room.

Louie went over to the bar and the attendant asked "*What's your pleasure* boss?"

"Give me some of your *BAD MEDICINE* whiskey." said Louie.

He sat at the bar in silence for awhile contemplating what the guitarist meant before he passed out "*I'll sleep when I'm dead.*" however, I don't think he will die. Because he does *work for the working man everyday,* I suppose that I'll have to pay him *blood money,* money for wages and to cover his medical expenses 'cos he was accidentally shot by me or there will be more *blood on blood* in the future.

If you *stick to your guns,* and *keep the faith* Louie and don't go *livin' on a prayer* you will be the *last man standing* at the end of the day." thought Louie.

"Give me another shot of your *BAD MEDICINE.*" said Louie to the barman.

It was while he was looking around at the patrons who were still there, he spotted another female.

"Come and *lay your hands on me* and *gimme some lovin' Charlene* and don't *you give love a bad name* either." demanded Louie. "Charlene, do *you want to make a memory* now?

For you, I would lay you on a *bed of roses* and hold you *in these arms.*"

11

Charlene walked over to Louie and while standing by his side she asked "Pookie, (Louie) why did you say to *Janie, don't take your love to town* and why did she say "*Someday I'll be Saturday night* and that *you give love a bad name?*"

Louie said "Don't you worry about that. You *just keep the faith* you have in me and I will give you a *diamond ring* if you just *lay your hands on me* while I hold you *in these arms*. *I'll be there for you* 'cos you were *born to be my baby* and we will start *livin' on a prayer.*"

Charlene then cuddled into Louie and whispered in his ear "You may be *just older* than me by a few years and I think it's a good idea that we start *livin' on a prayer*. *I'll be there for you* too and *I'd die for you*. Maybe someday I'll be Sunday night or was it *someday I'll be Saturday night*. Oh what's the difference, *I'll sleep when I'm dead* anyway so let's have a good time till then."

The patrons who had fled came back into the Entertainment Room and *Jumpin Jack Flash* came out onto the stage and said "Good evening ladies and gentlemen. Tonight *I'll sleep when I'm dead.*"

The crowd looked at him in a puzzling manner.

"Please don't let me be *misunderstood,* I mean that we will have *one wild night* so *raise your hands* and come and *bounce* on the floor to my latest hit tunes. Afterwards we can go *wild in the streets* and maybe you can end up being *wanted dead or alive* by your partner if you have one. Don't worry about all that *blood on blood* on the floor; it will be cleaned up shortly."

A woman approached me and said "Come, *lay your hands on me* and we will have the next dance. They are going to *let it rock* so let's get going for *I'll sleep when I'm dead*. Don't worry, you were not *born to be my baby* and I don't have my *love for sale* either. I am *just older* than you and *it's my life* so I'm not going to waste it by *livin' on a prayer* or doing anything that would make me *wanted dead or alive.*"

Louie whispered something to Charlene and then I heard her say "*Who says you can't go home? The distance* isn't that far. There you can *lay your hands on me* and *in these arms* you would never want to be *in and out of love* again. You would *never say goodbye* to me because *I'd die for you*. You were *born to be my baby* and you would want to *keep the faith* that you'll have in me.

12

You could also give me that *diamond ring* that you said you were going to give me. Yes Pookie, *someday I'll be Saturday night* but until then I will just stay here, for I'm *all about lovin you.*"

Janie walked away from the hotel in a *blaze of glory* saying "The *radio saved my life tonight* as I heard the announcer say *who says you can't go home?*

Everyday someone says, *who says you can't go home. These days,* there are so many people in a hurry that they say they will do things tomorrow and as you know tomorrow never comes.

I love this town and don't *say it isn't so* and *everyday* you can make someone feel good just by smiling and saying *have a nice day* to them.

It's my life and I never want to hear someone say to me again that *you give love a bad name* because I know that it's not true."

I had never paid attention to other people before but then I realized that they too had their own concerns, trials and tribulations to deal with. I had seen another part of life that I never knew existed.

The following morning I boarded the bus again, relieved to be leaving and wondered where the next place was and if it was as bad as the two towns that we had already visited.

A feint voice echoed from somewhere "*Blaze of glory, I'll be there for you* who cares?"

What I want to know is "WHO WILL SAVE NEW JERSEY?"

LOOKING BACK

This *Lost Highway* is never ending and this *dry county* is becoming so depressing. No green living vegetation anywhere, just brown withering life forms.

No wonder the people who lived in the previous towns felt like they were *livin' on a prayer* and needed to *keep the faith* because they would keep giving each other *bad medicine* all the time by saying stuff like "*You give love a bad name, someday I'll be Saturday night* or you are always *in and out of love.*" It seemed to me that their hearts were the things that were *wanted dead or alive* and although *everybody's broken* in one way or another, they all seemed to think that *love ain't nothing but a four letter word.*

Guano City was where there were all those *Wanted Dead Or Alive* posters hung all over the place including the one for the *runaway* who I haven't seen since I left there. Just about all the citizens there were *livin' on a prayer* and were trying so hard to *keep the faith.* I noticed that even the *good guys don't always wear white* and would say *someday I'll be Saturday night.*

I am still trying to figure out what they meant by that.

The one place I did find interesting was the saloon where they had the *Wanted Dead Or Alive* posters varnished along the bar and the unusual *BAD MEDICINE* brand of alcohols which tasted so horrible that it could make you *shout* so loud, that it would cause a *whole lot of leaving* from the other people who would think that they were in danger.

Everyday in that city you could hear people saying *you give love a bad name* or don't *you give love a bad name, who says you can't go home, you were born to be my baby, I'll sleep when I'm dead, this ain't a love song* and *it's my life.*

No-one ever said to someone else "*Have a nice day.*" It was always something negative said or it would be something related just for them.

When Louie said "*Janie, don't take your love to town*" he didn't want her to go because it meant that she would not have her *love for sale* to him anymore. Once he realized that he couldn't stop her from leaving and she did leave, it didn't take him long to *bounce* back and call for Charlene to be his next girlfriend.

14

Charlene never wanted to be *in and out of love* and she was *burning for love* from Louie. She accepted the *diamond ring* from him and began *livin' on a prayer* and *livin' in sin.* To start of with, she was *only lonely* but did not put her *love for sale* until she met Louie who thought that *love ain't nothing but a four letter word.* He did *treat her right* she gave him her *undivided* love and proved that she would *keep the faith* that she had in him.

Although we have just left his place, I heard from a fellow traveller that she had a *baby girl* to him and Louie seemed to change from being *wild in the streets* to not *livin' on a prayer* anymore. He stopped drinking any kind of *BAD MEDICINE* and became a good father.

He would constantly tell his daughter "You were *born to be my baby* and *I'll be there for you always.* If I had to *I'd die for you.*" He would also say to her "Never will *you give love a bad name* because your mother is a good person and will bring you up right. *It's my life* that had been messed up.

I was once *wanted dead or alive* and thought I'd go out in a *blaze of glory* for causing so much *blood on blood.* I was much younger then and thought that I should live it up as *I'll sleep when I'm dead.*

Then one day when I was riding across the *dry county* I said "*Hey God* please *lay your hands on me* for I am *wanted dead or alive* but I want to live not die. I am sorry for causing so much *blood on blood* and I *misunderstood* the meaning to *keep the faith.*

I gave myself up and did my time in jail. I am not proud of that but then I bought the hotel and built the *BAD MEDICINE* bar where I met your mother. Now you are here, I can *bounce* you on my knee and we can live a good life together."

I thought that *Jumpin Jack Flash* really settled the crowd down after the shooting and when he said *I'll sleep when I'm dead,* I wondered if he was thinking that he was going to be shot next. I think given the chance he would have had a good shot of *BAD MEDICINE* whiskey to calm himself down. At least he didn't say *someday I'll be Saturday night* because he was Saturday night, well the entertainment for the night.

I also thought the lady who asked me to dance was very nice although she seemed *just older* than me and the way she asked me was funny. I had never heard anyone ask for a dance by saying "Come, *lay your hands on me.*" I'll have to try that sometime and see if it works.

In each town there was a *whole lot of leaving* happening, *hearts breaking even* and others who were *livin' in sin* but they were all actually living on the *edge of a broken heart* and were taking *BAD MEDICINE* as they believed it to be *something for the pain* for a *cold hard heart.*

I heard a guy sitting in the seat in front of me say to the female sitting beside him "You can say *"This ain't a love song"* when you are heard *talkin' in your sleep.* Screaming out *you give love a bad name* and you weren't *born to be my baby* and say that love *ain't nothing but a kiss* because if you do, you would be telling a *lie to me."*

When I think of my girl, I think of a *woman in love.* One who was *born to be my baby* and who is *burning for love.* A woman, whilst lying *in these arms* in a *bed of roses,* would *lay your hands on me. I need your love* and I will *always run to you. I believe* that *love will stand when all else falls.*

It's my life and I *can't help falling in love,* even though I stood *staring at your window with a suitcase in my hand* as I leave after telling her that *I'll be there for you.* I can't help being *head over heels* in love with her. Sometimes I feel like I'm *livin' on a prayer* and I'm *all about loving you* but *I want to be loved* too.

If I was your mother I would tell you to *keep the faith* and *don't keep me wondering* as to whether you would *say it isn't so* that our love could grow. *These arms are open all night* and I want to hold you *till we ain't strangers anymore.* The last time that we talked, *every word was a piece of my heart* and I would not have said it *if I didn't love you. I get a rush* when I remember the time you said "That you will *always* love me and that you felt like you were *livin' on a prayer* as you laid *in these arms* in a *bed of roses."*

You said "If you *want to make a memory* please *don't leave me tonight* and *never say goodbye." Everyday* I thought that *we got it going on* but I *misunderstood* because you ended up leaving me and going away with *Joey.*

It's hard letting you go but then I realized that you will never *lay your hands on me* again and that *you give love a bad name* now and you thought that you had left in a *blaze of glory.* On *any other day* there would have been *blood on blood* for what you had done to me and remember when I said that *"I'll be there for you* ---- Well, forget it babe!

16

If I can't have your love, I will just leave this place forever and *who says you can't go home* to a place where you are wanted and loved. *It's my life* and I will live it by having a good time for *I'll sleep when I'm dead.*"

The *radio saved my life tonight* because I was able to get some reception whilst travelling on the bus and I was listening to a talk back station as one caller recalled how her deceased husband managed to find a way to get her to marry him.

She said "He said to me, you were *born to be my baby* and if you marry me, *I'll be there for you* and I would hold you *in these arms* forever. I don't think that *you give love a bad name.* He even said "*I'd die for you*" and he did. He pushed me out of the way of a drunk driver and was killed in doing so.

One day, not long before he died, he said to me "*You want to make a memory* and help me plant a *bed of roses* for you." I'm glad we made that garden for each time I go out and walk through it; I feel as if I'm still close to him and feel him in my heart. I no longer feel as if I am *livin' on a prayer* and I know that one day I'll join him in heaven and we will be together again."

Who says you can't go home and *these days* I can do what ever I like because *it's my life* but when will I get there, maybe the next place we stop will be home.

HALLELUJAH! We're leaving this dry desolate place but where we'll stop, only the driver knows.

"But WHO WILL SAVE NEW JERSEY?" I hear again and I look around at the passengers to see if I can find out who keeps asking that question.

17

THE FOUR PATHS

Whoa!

What kind of place was this?

After seeing nothing but desert, brown wilting trees and grass in the *dry county,* we had driven into a country side full of color. Everywhere green grass, trees and flowers of every kind and color was growing and clear running streams that stop suddenly; like at a border of some kind.

My mood had become brighter but I was still a bit hesitant to see what lay ahead.

What would the next place or town be like?

There are farms now and more houses so we must be approaching a town of some sorts. The driver pulled into a bus station and everyone on board was happy to get off. There was so much beauty there that I turned a full circle to take in the view.

Hey! Hang on a minute!

Where's the bus gone? It was there just a minute ago, and now it's disappeared, it has completely vanished and all in one turn of my body.

I walked out of the bus station and I looked at a *two story town,* yes, every building had two floors. I saw a child *bounce* a ball against a wall and I saw many people *dancing in the street.* I even saw a cat fussing over her kitten and meowing, it sounded like she was telling it that you were *born to be my baby* so I thought that I would go for a walk and look around the place.

The town was called Chelsea and the main street was named LITTLE *TOKYO ROAD.* I stopped a woman who was walking by and asked her why the people were dancing in the streets and she said "*Everyday* we celebrate the good things in life and at *midnight in Chelsea* we *let it rock.* We *shout* and become *wild in the streets* and hope that everyone else is *rockin' all over the world.* Yes, we have *one wild night.*"

I saw a *bed of roses* that was different from all the others that I had seen in the other towns and I asked the woman about them.

She looked at her watch and before dashing away she said that they were called the *Blaze of Glory* roses and when in full bloom they looked like a pool of *blood on blood* on the ground. She also said that years ago someone who was *livin' on a prayer* watered another bed of roses with *BAD MEDICINE* wine and killed the roses; so that bed was the only one left in town that looks like *blood on blood* when in full bloom. "Gotta run now, *Have a nice day*."

I also saw a different use for *Wanted Dead Or Alive* posters. On a large outdoor Notice Board one *Wanted Dead Or Alive* poster named all the activities that were happening in town that day and the other *Wanted Dead Or Alive* poster named where all the sales were happening so *just like a woman,* I guessed that's where she was dashing off to; to buy a *diamond ring* cheap.

I love this town and if *someday I'll be Saturday night,* whatever that means, I think that I'd like to be it, right here.

The sun was going down so I thought I had better get a meal from somewhere. I walked up the street and came across the "*SOMETHING FOR THE PAIN*" diner so I went in.

Curiously I asked the waiter about the name of the diner and he told me that when some people get hungry their stomachs hurt so hence the name and because of the large variety of meals and snacks on the menu, they would fix the pain. We also have *BAD MEDICINE* wine, juice, tea and coffee that you can have with the meal, but I don't suggest the wine.

The next minute a young man about twenty years old rushed into the diner and told the waiter "The *radio saved my life tonight* because the female announcer said "*Welcome to wherever you are* and get ready for the surprise of the night. The music store is going to be *open all night* and the three songs on special tonight are *I'LL SLEEP WHEN I'M DEAD, THIS AIN'T A LOVE SONG* and *YOU GIVE LOVE A BAD NAME*."

I am going to *keep the faith* and hope I am not *livin' on a prayer* that they are not sold out already. If I can get those songs I will stay awake all night and play them continuously for *I'll sleep when I'm dead*."

Then he rushed out again.

The waiter identified the young man as Tony and told me that his mother had kicked him out and told him not to come back because he was always bringing the wrong type of friends home who were a bad influence on his younger brother.

Then he said "Anyway, *who says you can't go home?*

My momma *always* told me that, you were *born to be my baby* and I will hold you *in these arms* anytime you want me to as *I'll be there for you* and I won't let *you give love a bad name*. Even though you say *"It's my life* and I can do what I want, I want you to know that you should *never say goodbye* and walk away from those who love you. Oh, don't let me be *misunderstood* because *these days* many children must learn to *keep the faith* and not start *livin' on a prayer.*"

Walking into the diner *Joey* said to his older brother Tony "Don't you dare *say it isn't so* and don't you dare *raise your hands* to me because if you do it will mean that *you give love a bad name*. You may be *just older* than me but *it's my life* and *with a little help from my friends* I may be able to travel down the *Lost Highway* to a *destination anywhere* and get a life of my own."

I left the diner without eating there and decided to keep walking through the town until I ventured into a park that had four paths leading from it, one went to the left, one went to the right, one went up a hill and one went down underground.

There was a rather large *bed of roses* surrounding the signpost that pointed in the four directions of the paths and written on each of the pointers was "LEFT, RIGHT, UP, DOWN, MAKE YOUR CHOICE AND FOLLOW THAT PATH".

Again I heard "But WHO WILL SAVE NEW JERSEY?"

PATH ONE

I chose to follow the path that went to the left first and after a short walk I found myself in front of a café. A sign hung over the door that read *"WELCOME TO WHEREVER YOU ARE.* COME IN AND HAVE A REST*"*.

I thought that this would be a good place for a meal and a cool drink as I never had anything in the last diner and I was rather hungry and thirsty.

After going inside I noticed that on the top shelf hidden behind some other bottles were *BAD MEDICINE* whiskey and *BAD MEDICINE* wine.

The menus for the food and drinks were printed on colorful *Wanted Dead Or Alive* posters and on the wall closest to the back of the dining room was a large mirror that was mounted in another *Wanted Dead Or Alive* poster made from wood. The café had three other customers sitting at tables when I walked in.

The waiter took my order and a short time later brought my meal to the table that was next to a large window. Under the window I noticed the same *bed of roses* that I had seen in the last town, the *Blaze of Glory* roses that when in full bloom looked like a pool of *blood on blood* on the ground.

Whilst I was eating, I noticed a young man outside sitting on a park bench opposite the café and he seemed to be crying softly. He had something in his arms but from where I was sitting, I couldn't see what it was.

I finished my meal, went outside and over to the young man to see if he needed any assistance. We started talking then he said *"My guitar lies bleeding in my arms* and that's why I'm upset."

I didn't understand what he meant but before I could ask him to explain himself, he carried on telling me of the *ballad of youth.* Then I got the *confessions of a teenage lycanthrope* and that his *papa was a rolling stone.*

He also said "I am *chained* to my *father's sins* and that the *law of the jungle* says that I will *inherit the dead* and I will be *damned.* The *story of my life* is *complicated."*

21

Hey! *I don't like Mondays* at the best of times, even though it is Monday, but is this kid for real or is he tripping on some *bad medicine* and *livin' on a prayer?*

The young man looked at me solemnly and said "The *radio saved my life tonight* because I realized that I am *only lonely* and that I find the *hardest part of the night* for me is to *keep the faith* and stop *livin' on a prayer*. Then this voice came over the radio and asked "Would *you give love a bad name* or were you *born to be my baby?*"

I thought about both questions and said to myself that I needed to *keep the faith* and forget *livin' on a prayer* as it will get me nowhere. *It's my life* and I want *something more* than being *wanted dead or alive*. Papa once told me that we're *blood on blood* and our type of people, are always *wanted dead or alive,* preferably dead and when we change our appearance we become *ugly.*"

I thought that "*If I was your mother* I would take you *in these arms* and tell you that *I'll be there for you* even when you fall *in and out of love*. Some days a mother's love *ain't nothing but a kiss* and a dose of *bad medicine*. Other days she will say to you *Thank you for loving me* as much as I love you."

Then he said "*Someday I'll be Saturday night* and I would be able to *shout* to the world "*I got the girl* of my dreams who lives around the corner from my house." and I would say to her "Don't *you give love a bad name* as you *lay your hands on me* while *I learn to love* you. You were *born to be my baby* and *I can't help falling in love* with you. I want to hold you *in these arms* and *I'll be there for you* but most importantly *I'd die for you* if I had to for I'm *all about lovin' you*. But I am *livin' on a prayer* here because *she don't know me*.

Hey God, please don't let me be *damned, give me something to believe in*. I don't want to be *knockin' on heavens door* or end up on the *right side of wrong* and have to live out in the *dry county*.

You know the *story of my life* is *complicated*. I would *keep the faith* and *I believe* in you and I want to *thank you for loving me* because never do *you give love a bad name. The fire inside* me would *never say die* so as *it's my life* I will live it to the fullest and then *I'll sleep when I'm dead.*"

I may be *just older* than this kid but I am having trouble in understanding why in every place I've been to so far have had people saying the same things over and over again, like *keep the faith, lay your hands on me, livin' on a prayer* and *you give love a bad name* or don't *you give love a bad name* or *I'll sleep when I'm dead* or *someday I'll be Saturday night.*

What does it all mean and are they trying to tell me something?

Maybe I'm the one who is being *misunderstood* or maybe *with a little help from my friends* I could begin to understand what they mean.

Everyday I want to *shout "It's my life* and I want you to *lay your hands on me* and help me understand what's going on because I don't want anyone to tell me that *you give love a bad name.* On *any other day I'll sleep when I'm dead."*

OH!!! What did I say? I don't know. I'm so confused.

This will be the *last night* that I'll stay here because *this ain't a love song* but a sad song and a confusing place to be.

As I walked back up the path to the signpost, I saw a different sign stuck in the ground that read "IF YOU WANT A PRICK THEN LAY DOWN IN THIS *BED OF ROSES* AND YOU WILL GET ONE*".*

Now what does that mean or is it something else to confuse me more?

When I finally reached the signpost, two other people were standing there talking. The lady just finished saying that she saw Earth Angel David and his mates disappearing down the down path.

Then they looked at me with a puzzling stare and asked *"Why aren't you dead?*

A few other people saw you talking to a young kid and told us that many other people who had met the same young kid never came back because he went crazy *on a full moon* and killed them."

Then I heard that question again "WHO WILL SAVE NEW JERSEY?"

PATH TWO

While I was standing near the signpost trying to figure out again which way to go next, that question I kept hearing "Who will save New Jersey?" came back into my head.

I wondered who kept asking the question and why; do they want me to save New Jersey and if so, how? Why does New Jersey need to be saved anyway?

I made up my mind and thought that this time I would go - up and see if it was the path that would lead me out of there and back towards home.

Again it was just a short walk to a road.

Painted on the actual road was "THIS IS *TOKYO ROAD*. IT WILL TAKE YOU TO YOUR *DESTINATION ANYWHERE*. IF YOU WANT TO GET ON, I WILL AT LEAST TAKE YOU UP THE MOUNTAIN".

As soon as I stepped onto the road and it started moving up, towards the mountain. I started to panic and I tried to get off but I couldn't; I was stuck in place.

Once I reached the top, a man came forward and said that he was the *King of the mountain*. I asked him where the road actually went and he said that it went down a bit (he pointed to the other side of the mountain) then it double backed on itself and eventually joined the *Lost Highway*. *It's a long road* to travel. The town of Chelsea named its main street LITTLE *TOKYO ROAD* as it branched off from the main road that runs through here.

The King asked me if I was *wanted dead or alive* because if I was, there may be some *blood on blood* later as some of the other lads may try to collect the *blood money* that was being offered for my capture.

I told him "No." and asked why it was called *blood money* instead of a reward.

He told me that many years ago when his *papa was a rolling stone,* there were so many people *wanted dead or alive* that the only way for them to be captured was to shoot them.

The criminals, who had turned to the *right side of wrong* and were *livin' on a prayer,* would then be brought back into town where they

24

would either be buried or treated for gun shot wounds with a lot of *bad medicine*. There was usually a lot of *blood on blood* so hence the name Blood Money.

The *heroes* who captured the criminals would then have a few *BAD MEDICNE* whiskeys and go *wild in the streets* for a few hours before heading out again. Sometimes the shoot outs came down to whoever was the *last man standing* and if the criminal was, he would *runaway* and was *damned*."

The King then said "*The boys are back in town* after they had been out in the *Broken Promise Land* for the past few days *crashing kites*. They will be *wild in the streets* tonight. Come on let's go to the pub and join in their fun."

I said "I know that I am a *stranger in this town* so I will *keep the faith* that I am not *misunderstood* and mistaken for a criminal on a previous *Wanted Dead Or Alive* poster."

As we started walking the King assured me that I would be safe with him and for me not to worry but we seemed to be walking in circles through a small forest until we finally came to the pub that had a *bed of roses* growing along one side of the entrance path. On the other side of the path were plants growing that I didn't recognise or knew the names of them; however their fragrance was so nice and calming.

It wasn't a very large pub however it had a cozy setting inside. A fire in the large bar room raged in a *blaze of glory* and the music being played made it feel like a *room full of blues*.

There was a *back door frenzy* and shouts of "*Ride cowboy ride* and buddy *I'll sleep when I'm dead*." The King explained to me that outside there was a Buckin' Bronco machine and men would get on it and ride until the *last man standing* was decided.

A woman came over and the King made the *intro* and said that she was *Miss Fourth of July*, our hostess for the evening and would give us her *undivided* attention. He said that although she had *love for sale* she doesn't give *bad medicine* and won't let *you give love a bad name*. Sometimes she is a *thorn in my side* but she *always* makes me feel as good as I do at Christmas and really *I wish everyday could be like Christmas*.

Miss July said "*Don't you believe him. All men are freaks* in their own way around here, except you; you seem like real *flesh and bone*. Most of them here are *livin' on a prayer* and think that *we got it going on.*

You wanna *lay your hands on me* so *in these arms* we could do a slow dance and we can talk some more. I like the King very much and wish that he was *born to be my baby* but I think that I may be just *livin' on a prayer,* hoping that he would feel the same way about me."

Then I heard yelling and *"YOU GIVE LOVE A BAD NAME, YOU GIVE LOVE A BAD NAME, YOU GIVE LOVE A BAD NAME"* and looked around wondering where it was coming from.

Miss July said "Oh there they go again. The boys are shouting messages down Echo Valley again and then will wait to see if someone further down the valley would hear them and answer them back. Usually they say *"It's my life* and *Someday I'll be Saturday night* and *I'll sleep when I'm dead."*

One time they did receive an answer back. Someone down the valley echoed back *IT'S MY LIFE* and I would *KEEP THE FAITH* and would never be *LIVIN' ON A PRAYER."*

When I finally sat down after the dancing, the King said "Fishing is a *social disease* around here and tomorrow the boys and me are going *up the river. You want to make a memory* and come with us?

There are many fish there that are *wanted dead or alive* by the boys so we will be *stringin' a line* in the *Black Magic River* near where the *river runs dry.*

You may have to wear a warm jacket 'cos *wild is the wind* up there. Afterwards we'll come back here and have a drink the boys call *bad medicine; something for the pain* of telling everyone about *the one that got away.* If you *keep the faith* then you may be *lucky* enough to catch something."

Miss July said "Even though *I don't like Mondays, someday I'll be Saturday night* and *I'll be there for you* if you want me too. Oh, sorry, please don't let me be *misunderstood* for using our own lingo, I mean that we'll party like there's no tomorrow because *I'll sleep when I'm dead.* If you *stick to your guns* then the chances that *you give a bad name* are very slim."

26

I apologized and declined the offer for them to *hook me up* to go fishing with them and said that I wanted to get back because all I really wanted to do is just get home.

Miss July said "*Everyday,* you get *just older* and *who says you can't go home* when you feel the need to, so come and *lay your hands on me* and give me a hug before you go. You are welcome here anytime you want to come back."

The King said he was sorry too that I declined to go fishing and he said he understood how I felt. He drove me down the mountain and directed me back to the signpost.

As I left I thought "*It's my life* and if I *keep the faith* and don't start *livin' on a prayer* I will be fine. So far every town has had a *bed of roses* in it. I wondered why that was."

"WHO WILL SAVE NEW JERSEY?" asked the voice again.

Where is that voice coming from? It's starting to annoy me.

PATH THREE

Well, that wasn't such a bad place to visit but I think that I am going to have to experience a lot more before I get out of here and back home.

I thought that I would try the path that went right next. I could see the road from the path and I guessed it was the other part of *Tokyo Road* and a sign that read TO *NEUROTICA*. Population Unknown

Now, that town was a strange one, it was mostly a *two story town* but it had some caves on one side of town where the *Platinum Heroes* lived. *Wild is the wind* that blew across the *edge of a broken heart,* past a big cave on the other side of town where the *man with a dragon* lived.

Then I heard *"YOU GIVE LOVE A BAD NAME. YOU GIVE LOVE A BAD NAME, YOU GIVE LOVE A BAD NAME"* and realized that they were the messages the boys had sent down Echo Valley.

A reply was sent back, "YOU ARE NOW *WANTED DEAD OR ALIVE.* YOU ARE NOW *WANTED DEAD OR ALIVE.* YOU ARE NOW *WANTED DEAD OR ALIVE."*

I had a small giggle to myself when I heard the reply. I couldn't help but notice a *Wanted Dead Or Alive* poster that was pinned to a big Oak tree but it only had the words *"GET THE GEEK"* on it, no picture.

From some people passing by, I heard that the *runaway* had moved in with the *rich man living in a poor man's house* and she was no longer the *devil on the run* but she would still give you a *fever* because *evil is hot.* Even though they were *living in sin,* the rich man said to her "Me, a *fool, fool, fool.* NO. When *I'll play the fool for you,* it will be --- NEVER. You're *livin' on a prayer* and *you give love a bad name* and you *lie to me."*

The *Platinum Heroes* came into town that evening and began to run *wild in the streets* when a *satellite* crossed the sky in a *blaze of glory* because in the *next 100 years* it would only happen once more.

They said mean things to the townsfolk like "If you *lay your hands on me* I will *kick your ass* or *scratch my itch* if you don't want to live in *fear* or be *damned.* We are always drinking *BAD MEDICINE* whiskey and our caves are *out of bounds* to everyone that we don't take there.

We don't care if you are *livin' on a prayer,* if you *keep the faith* or you *lie to me;* but, if you can get us a supply of *BAD MEDICINE* whiskey or

BAD MEDICINE rum then you could become one of our friends and help us get through the *hardest part of the night* when we visit *Garageland;* you know that place where everyone lives in garages." said one of the *heroes.*

Although it was *99 in the shade,* the *Harlem rain* didn't seem to cool the air down much; it had only watered the *bed of roses* after the brief shower had past over.

The man with the dragon came into town to hear the *Ballad of Youth* and the *Lullaby for Two Moons* that were being played at the *Midnight Voodoo* Club that evening.

In the club we had a drink, some unusual type of nibbles and sat and talked a bit and then referring to the song being played at the time, he said *"This ain't a love song* you know, it's *The Chanukah Song* and some people believe it to be like *Prayer 94.*

It seems that *hard times come easy* for anyone who was on the *downside of love. Livin' on a prayer* didn't work either as you had to have *something to believe in. In these arms* you need someone to hold onto and will love you in return for your love." he said as he took hold of both of my arms in his hands.

Then he pointed to a group of women and said "They are the *summer of dreams.* Yes, *the ones with the angel eyes.* If you could *kidnap an angel,* you could live in true happiness.

Everybody dies at some stage in their lives as I did once and a *miracle* happened when I was *kissed by an angel* and she stayed long enough to *love me back to life.* I think that she was *born to be my baby."*

One of the women with angel eyes came up to me and made her *intro* by saying *"You want to make a memory* before you *rest in peace,* because the one *who said it would last forever* was *all talk, no action.* He thought that *someday I'll be Saturday night* and that he was *born to be my baby.* But he was wrong."

She looked over my shoulder at someone and her face went pale before turning and walking quickly back to her table.

I stayed for about an hour and as I walked to the door to leave, I saw a *naked* man approach a mature aged woman sitting in the corner and thought *"Thank God she's blind* because she can't see what he looks like."

There was a *whole lot of leaving* once the other patrons saw the man.

The owner of the club was not very happy either when he saw the man and shouted to him "*Run run Rudolph* because *my guitar lies bleeding in my arms* and I have to fix it, before I'll be able to bring you down with a *shot through the heart*. You are just *livin' on a prayer* and because I think you're too ugly to shoot, stuff and mount on the wall, you had better *runaway* quickly."

As Rudolph took off running he said "*It's my life* you want to mess with. Don't you dare *lay your hands on me* or *hook me up* on your wall. You don't have to shoot me to kill me for *I'll sleep when I'm dead* and then no one will bother me again. Just you *keep the faith* that I don't come after you."

"*Everyday* there is someone *livin' on a prayer* and looking to take *something for the pain*. Please *don't keep me wondering* whether being *without love* from a special person would make someone put up their *love for sale* for *one wild night* or go *wild in the streets*." said the young female sitting at the table with the owner.

She waited for a moment then she carried on saying "I was listening to the radio playing in a smaller room of the club for awhile tonight and I know that the *radio saved my life tonight* when I heard someone say "*Who says you can't go home? These days* there is a *whole lot of leaving* of people from their families. They were usually too busy chasing life and if they were asked to slow down a bit they would say "I can't at the moment but *I'll sleep when I'm dead.*"

On *any other day* I would have prayed out loud "*Hey God*, I know that *it's my life*. I will *keep the faith* and *never say goodbye* to you. You *have a nice day* now." but I couldn't do that there and then.

As I passed back out of the door, I was surprised to find myself standing at the signpost again. I wanted to pinch myself so I'd wake up as my trip had been pretty weird up until then.

I was feeling a bit hungry and tried to think about my last meal but I couldn't recall any food I had eaten only the unusual type of nibbles that I had just had that could have made me feel like I did. What were those strange nibbles...mushrooms!!!!

Oh no. There's that question again "WHO WILL SAVE NEW JERSEY?" Where is it coming from?

30

PATH FOUR

Well; standing back at the sign post I had only one direction left to go – down.

So there I went.

There was only *one light burning* as I ventured *underground* and the light was so bright that it lit all the way down. I heard the *bells of freedom* ringing and someone *bang a drum* as I entered the opening at the bottom.

There were two towns Graceland and *Garageland* and they were a *mirror image* of each other; however, I thought that Graceland might be *just older* by a little bit. I was surprised to see the *Blaze of Glory bed of roses,* the ones that looked like *blood on blood* when they were in full bloom growing everywhere.

I found a diner where I went in for a burger and a coffee because I was just so hungry. All the menus were printed on *Wanted Dead Or Alive* posters and pictures of different foods were stuck to wooden *Wanted Dead Or Alive* poster frames. There was also a bottle of *BAD MEDICINE* wine hidden behind the counter on a lower shelf.

After ordering my meal, I was sitting in a booth enjoying the peace and quiet when I heard the waitress carry on a conversation with a young man sitting at the counter.

Waitress: "So what happened then Billy?"

Billy: "Well, *Sylvia's mother* said to her, I heard you *talkin' in your sleep* and you said that *love ain't nothing but a four letter word* and that *love lies* 'cos *you give love a bad name* by taking all that *bad medicine* and you are always *livin' on a prayer.*"

Waitress: "So now her *dirty little secret* has just come out. What will her mother do now?"

Billy: "Well, her mother wanted to *tear the house down*, because Sylvia had *fallen from Graceland* but instead she is going to take her to church to see if they can find her *undiscovered soul.*"

31

Waitress: "You know at their church they say *Hallelujah, Raise your hands* to the Lord so he can *hear our prayer*. You have to *keep the faith* as your soul is *wanted dead or alive*."

Billy: "They also say *this ain't a love song* so *let it rock* as we ask the Lord to help all those who are *livin' on a prayer* and we shall *save a prayer* for all those who seem to keep falling *in and out of love*...Like me".

Waitress: "You have my *sympathy*. You must be a *stranger to love* and sometimes when we fall in love we get *more than we bargained for*."

Billy: "Yes, but I'm *learning how to fall* and how to *bounce* back again."

Waitress: "Hey, did you hear about *Bobby's girl?*"

She poured more coffee into Billy's cup.

Billy: "No."

Waitress: "Well, you know how they had that fight and he said to her *you give love a bad name?*"

Billy: "Yes."

Waitress: "Bobby told her that she *misunderstood* the situation and then said to her *don't stop loving me now* and *don't leave me tonight*. He told her that *no one does it like you* and then said that you were *born to be my baby*."

Billy: "Then what happened?"

Waitress: "She said "Please *don't do that to me any more* and you have to work out *what you want* for the rest of your life and don't say that *someday I'll be Saturday night* for it will never happen."

Billy: "How did he take that?"

Waitress: "He said that *it's hard letting you go* and *I just want to be your man*. I want us to talk and work things out *till we ain't strangers anymore*."

32

Billy: "But didn't that happened months ago! What about it?"

Waitress: "I have just found out that there is *big love* between them and
           they are *undivided* now. He told her *I could make a living out
           of loving you* and then gave her a *diamond ring* and said *thank
           you for loving me.*"

Billy: "So, they're getting married then?"

Waitress: "Yes, in the *summertime* at the *Chapel of Love* on the banks
           of the *River of Love* that flows along side the *Lost Highway*.
           Do you think that they will live together till then?"

Billy: "No. I don't think her mother will let them and besides he is
           just older than her so it wouldn't look good for either of them.
           Other townsfolk would think that she was only with him
           because she would have her *love for sale*.
           Are you going to *the ceremony?*"

Waitress: "I think so, *I believe* that the band *Birds of a Feather* may
           play at the reception and *I get a rush* every time I hear them
           play, especially the song *Rockin' All Over The World*."

Billy: "You know that this makes me feel like I do at Christmas and
           I wish everyday could be like Christmas so I could be as
           happy now. Well maybe *someday* so I'll *keep the faith* and try
           not to be *livin' on a prayer*."

Waitress: "*Someday might just be tonight* because *all I wanna do is you*
           to ask me out."

Billy: "I didn't know that you felt that way about me?"

Waitress: "I have for a long time and I can't wait any longer for you to
           ask me out. I *can't help falling in love* with you and I am
           certain that you were *born to be my baby* and I am *all about
           loving you.*"

Billy: "To be honest, I have *always* wanted to take you *in these
           arms* and tell you that *I'll be there for you*."

Waitress: "Billy, are you saying that you may buy me a *diamond ring*
           one day? I don't want to be *misunderstood* for saying that but
           I don't want to be *livin' on a prayer* for the rest of my life
           either."

Billy: "Look, the *radio saved my life tonight* because after changing stations I heard somebody say *Hey God* is it wrong for me to have *one wild night* before I get married for I know that *I'll sleep when I'm dead* and that made me think about my life and what I want to do with it."

Waitress: "*We got it going on* and don't *say it isn't so*. If we can go *the distance* and *never say goodbye* then neither of us would say to each other *you give love a bad name* but only that never do *you give love a bad name*.
Will you go with me to Sylvia's wedding?"

Billy: "Yes, I'll go and we should *have a nice day.*
Hey, do *you want to make a memory* with me when you get off work?"

Waitress: "OK, why not. I finish in half an hour so why don't you just wait for me."

I finished the last of my coffee and left the diner. I just wanted to go home myself.

The road went one way and beside the curb was a sign that said "*Who says you can't go home* in *fast cars* along the *Lost Highway.*"

So I started to thumb a ride.

As the cars whistled past I heard someone yell out "WHO WILL SAVE NEW JERSEY?"

Then a limo pulled over and the driver got out and opened the door for me to get into the back seat with the female occupant.

ON THE ROAD

As the driver opened the door he said "*Hello, My name is Huey.*"

I climbed into the back section of the limo and sitting on a long plush cushion was a very beautiful woman. *If God was a woman* then she would be her.

The woman introduced herself as the *Queen of New Orleans* and asked if I would like a drink. She said it was not like that *Bitter Wine* that most people drank. She asked me where I was heading to and I told her that I was trying to get home.

Then she said something very profound. "I was born in *Novocaine* just outside *Memphis* where I grew up. *Maybe someday* I'll go back there; however, *who says you can't go home* any time you want to. Because *Memphis lives in me,* when I want to go home, all I have to do is look into my heart and I'll be there."

I thought she's right and if *Memphis lives in me* or the town where I was born then any *nobody* like me could go home anytime they wanted to because some people say that home is where the heart is.

As we were cruising along the road the *radio* was playing blues music and the Queen surprised me by saying "*Everybody wants to be black on a Saturday night* so they can go into the special Black Clubs to listen to this kind of music but on *any other day* they don't care what color they are."

When I looked at her face, I saw a deep sense of sorrow in her eyes when she said "A lot of people say *someday I'll be Saturday night* but they are only living in their *summer of dreams.* We all say cruel things to each other, and then we try to find *something for the pain* and a way of *taking it back* and don't *say it isn't so* for I have done it myself."

Then she said in a very sad tone "The *story of my life* is a story of struggle, discrimination and heartache. When I was young, *rockin' in the free world* was not allowed amongst my people as we were slaves. One day I decided to *runaway* and *with a little help from my friends* I did it even though we knew that we would be in serious trouble if I was caught.

Whilst on the run, I met a very nice white man and he traded me with one of his own servants to my old master. My new master's name was *Joey* and he ended up freeing me by marrying me.

It was allowed where we lived and we used to go out and *ride the night away* during the balmy summers.

He would tell me many times, "I know that you must have been *born to be my baby* and that *I'd die for you* and because of our mixed marriage we are *livin' on a prayer*." Then on one *silent night* he gave me this *diamond ring* and just after that two men who were *wanted dead or alive* rode up to our front porch from the direction of *Tokyo Road*.

They had an argument with my husband then shot him and as he lay dying in my arms he said "*Every word was a piece of my heart* that I ever spoke to you. You know that I love you and never did *you give love a bad name* to me and I want to *thank you for loving me*. I will *never say goodbye* to you because we will meet again also I knew that *someday I'll be Saturday night* but I didn't think that it would be this soon."

Everyday I miss him and I will *always* love him and be grateful for what he did for me because he made me the *Queen of New Orleans*. *Only in my dreams* can we be together again without having to be *livin' on a prayer*."

Huey informed the Queen over the intercom that he had just received a phone call from *Miss Fourth of July* saying that she and *Captain Crash and the Beauty Queen from Mars* were at the club *Destination Anywhere* and would meet her at *midnight in Chelsea* by the big fountain the following evening and would she please notify them upon her arrival before attending the party.

"Huey, please pull into the *Interlude* Club up ahead. It is *open all night* and *the distance* that we have travelled today must be tiring for you so you can have some rest before we continue on."

Once we had arrived at the club, Huey opened the door for us to get out and once she was out of the limo the Queen said to me "You may *lay your hands on me* and take my arm." and as we walked along the path into the club, I noticed a very old tombstone surrounded by flowers that looked like the *Blaze of Glory* roses that when in full bloom looked like a *blood on blood* patch on the ground.

The tombstone read "I said *I'LL SLEEP WHEN I'M DEAD*."

In the club I saw some people drinking *BAD MEDICINE* whiskey,

BAD MEDICINE rum and followed by a shot of *Tequila* as it took the bad taste of the rum and whiskey away.

We stayed there for a few hours so that Huey could have a really good rest before we started down the road again and also that the Queen was able to walk around and stretch her legs before having to sit down again in the limo.

As went started back down the *Lost Highway* the Queen said "*What you want* from life is usually different from what you get. Don't you agree?"

I said "*These days, everybody's broken* in their own particular way and *all I want is everything* to work out for me to have *a good life* and *with a little help from my friends* it may just happen. When you get down, you usually find *100 reasons* to *bounce* back and all you have to do is act on them.

Who says you can't go home when you are *only lonely* and you need a familiar, loving person to tell you that never do *you give love a bad name*. That would also bring you *one step closer* to bouncing back."

The Queen said "My sister pleads with me every year, *please come home for Christmas*. We need to talk and spend time together *till we ain't strangers anymore*. I don't know whether I want a *second chance* to get close to the family again because *the price of love* is too high. *I get a rush* just thinking about it yet I still don't know if I should go as *she don't know me* anymore."

I thought that *any woman like you* would jump at the chance, for how could *you give love a bad name* by not going.

We sat in silence for awhile and I wondered why I was travelling through all these different places and meeting all these different people. Then the *radio saved my life tonight* as I listened to the callers asking "*Why aren't you dead?*"

Other callers were saying that the *temptation* for people to try and *save the world* was enormous. *Change don't come easy* and when he's ready *Father Time* will put the world into a *golden slumber* and anyway *who said it would last forever?*

Do *you want to make a memory* for someone else? If you do then just smile and tell them to *have a nice day* because *these days* not many people would think of doing that, let alone do it."

37

Huey announced that their destination was just two miles up the road.

Just before the Queen turned off the radio I heard that question again. "WHO WILL SAVE NEW JERESEY?"

When I told the Queen about how I keep hearing the question that just came across the radio, she looked at me strangely and said "What question?"

Am I the only person who hears it?

THE PARTY

The closer we got to our destination, the noisier it got. The Queen explained to me that there was a *birthday* party in progress.

When I asked her whose birthday, she looked at me and said "Who knows, it's always somebody's birthday. The party has been going for the past fifty years and will still be going for the *next 100 years*.

You had better *get ready* for *one wild night* after another. The town has an *open door policy* so you can come and go as you please and nobody will be *damned* for being here.

Huey this time don't park on the *bed of roses*."

Huey pulled the limo to a stop, and then opened the door for us. When I got out all I could see was an *endless horizon* of people. There were people doing cartwheels and going *head over hills* but they looked like they were having fun.

The Queen told Huey to go and have a good time, then she turned to me and said "He turns into *crazy little Huey* now and believes he isn't *livin' on a prayer*. Come, I'll show you around a bit."

Before he left Huey said "Don't forget madam, you are to meet *Captain Crash and the Beauty Queen from Mars* and the others at midnight."

As we walked we saw people going *wild in the streets;* others were standing around an elderly man who seemed to look *just older* than the Queen and he was telling them about the *Legend of the Toxic Avenger*.

We walked to a large barn and went in and I saw *Captain Crash and the Beauty Queen from Mars* dancing the *Netherworld Waltz*. We stayed for a short while before there was a *whole lot of leaving* as the people made their way to the paddle steamer for a trip *up the river* while the band played a *Lullaby for Two Moons* and the pianist was going to give a *Keyboard solo*.

Miss Fourth of July came up to us and said "This is *my big French boyfriend*. He is *nobody's hero* really but he is my *superman tonight*. We are going to *rock and roll* and *twist and shout* tonight and he will *save the last dance for me*."

Then she disappeared with him and the rest of the crowd, so we left too.

We heard that at *midnight in Chelsea* they were going to *let it rock* and the Queen said "Do you want to *raise your hands, shout* out *Hallelujah* and get down for some *hot toxic love?*"

I said "Why not. Just *start me up* and *hook me up* and let's get going."

The Queen said "Well, *get ready* for some *good times*. The *hardest part of the night* will be trying to keep up with everything and *not fade away*. Yes, we are likely to become like everyone else and go *wild in the streets* and tonight it doesn't matter if *you give love a bad name* because no-one cares. Anyway I have to meet some other friends there."

As we were going over to Chelsea in a horse drawn open carriage, I noticed two people standing next to a notice board that had two notices on them. Both were made from a copy of a *wanted dead or alive* poster. One read "Your body is *wanted dead or alive* at any party, any where, any time." The other read "*HAPPY BIRTHDAY TO ALEC*".

The *runaway* seemed to be shouting at *Joey*. She yelled "I'm not the *thief of hearts* you are. *You tore my heart out* when you deserted me at the Mystery Train Station. That was *the last night* I saw you until I found you here."

Joey then replied "You don't have to shout at me. You know that partying is a *social disease* here and I had to take the *last chance train* to make it here on time. I couldn't find you to ask if you wanted to come with me. You know that I have always considered you as being *born to be my baby* and I always want you to *lay your hands on me*."

It was nearly midnight when *Southern Belle* rushed up to the Queen and said "I'm glad I've found you. The *radio saved my life tonight* 'cos I completely forgot about the party until I heard the announcement on the radio. *It's my life* and tonight I just want you to *raise your hands* and *hook me up* until *we got it going on*."

The Queen got the driver to stop so that Southern Belle could get in the carriage.

We finally arrived in Chelsea and the Queen and Southern Belle went looking for some *crazy love* leaving me sitting alone on a park bench.

I thought I saw *Jumpin Jack Flash* streak past *naked* but it wasn't, it was the *runaway* and *Joey* on bikes that would *bounce* along as you peddled them.

40

The colored woman, April saw me and asked "Can I sit in the *seat next to you?*" She said she noticed me with the Queen and told me to be careful.

When I asked her what she meant by that, she just looked at me and whispered "I'll explain soon but first *we gotta get out of this place.*" She took my hand and we left.

We walked for a short while and came across an empty park bench in a quiet area. We sat down and April told me that although she was born in Memphis, it didn't matter where she travelled; she could always go home because *Memphis lives in me* and I only have to look in my heart to go there. She then told me that the Queen's real name was *Wildflower*.

I said that the Queen had said the same thing about Memphis in the limo coming here.

April said "We were both *made in America* but *she's a mystery* and *she doesn't know me* even though *she's my sister.*"

Rosie ran past us yelling "There's a *whole lot of leaving* everywhere as everyone is going to *Tonk's Place* because *Mr. Bluesman* is filling a *room full of blues* and is going to play a *Guitar solo. This ain't a love song* that he'll be playing, but you will get the blues *fever* just listening to him.

Misunderstood will be doing the *introduction* like she used to do in her *glory days* when she was known as *Brown Sugar*.

We got it going on down there and we'll keep going *till the walls come down.* I'm going to live it up for now for *I'll sleep when I'm dead.*"

April then looked me in the eyes and said "Even though *you had me from hello,* you had better *lay your hands on me* and give me a hug. You will never be the *last man standing* so go, and have your *last cigarette* and catch the *Homebound Train.* Remember, if you *never say goodbye* you can always *come back.* If you don't come back, then remember us *when we were beautiful.*"

I gave her a hug and walked to the station.

I walked past a strange sign that read "I knew I was *Livin' On A Prayer* and I did *Keep The Faith* and I knew that *I'll Sleep When I'm Dead;* well, don't try to wake me for I am sleeping well."

I also saw more people on the bikes that would *bounce* down *Tokyo Road* as you peddled them.

From somewhere over the noise, I heard, yes, you guessed it, the question "WHO WILL SAVE NEW JERSEY?"

HOME COMING

The train was ready for departure when I arrived at the station. I sat in my seat and looked out the window and as we pulled away from the station I thought about all the things that I had been through and how they seemed to be like *Hollywood dreams.*

All I want is everything to go back to normal but somehow I don't think it will because I have seen and been involved in many things that seemed so unbelievable but real.

I had been in towns that had been *open all night* and where the citizens would have *one wild night* and go *wild in the streets.* They made you want to *raise your hands* and they gave you a hope that everyone is *rockin' all over the world.*

When the question arose about *who says you can't go home,* the citizens of the different places gave you a different answer each time but it all came down to you, to what you wanted to do. You're the one who says you can't because you are the *runaway* and *the distance* is the only barrier you put on yourself by making excuses not to go.

When I get home I will have to write a *letter to a friend* or two and tell them all about these experiences. I will tell them *what a wonderful world* we live in and for them to *shout* out *America the beautiful.* I will also tell them that if they have someone special in their lives they should tell them *everyday* that you were *born to be my baby* so *I'll be there for you* and I want to hold you *in these arms* forever.

These days, ordinary people think that they are *unbreakable* but they're not, they're only *livin' on a prayer;* besides many of them are just *lonely* and in their *secret dreams* they think that *love will stand when all else falls.*

We weren't born to follow so *starting all over again* is making me feel *just older,* old enough to know that *every beat of my heart* will keep me *rockin' in the free world. Everyday* you *gotta have a reason* to *breathe* and say *I can love* but you must also remember to *live before you die. I want you* to know that wherever you go *you're not alone.* You need to have a *little bit of soul* and *something to believe in.*

"Hey God, you know that there are times when *I speak to Jesus* and I read your book, known in many religions as The Bible.

You say in your book "*Have a little faith in me* and you must *keep the faith* for *help* will come and a remedy will be given that will be *something for the pain*. You also say that *these arms are open all night* for all those who are *livin' on a prayer* and for those who are not. *I believe* that you do give all people *something to believe in*.

I am just a Big Green Freak and from the people I have met it hasn't made a difference and the places that I have just been through makes me want to let you *lay your hands on me* and *make me believe* in you even more. I want to *thank you for loving me* and I do believe that you will be the *last man standing* when the end comes. I, myself have been *livin' on a prayer* and feel that your *undivided* love will *love me back to life*. Lord, please believe me when I say that *every word was a piece of my heart*."

A blonde haired man sitting in the seat in front of me said "*You can sleep while I dream* but if *you want to make a memory* you have to *stand up* and say to those close to you "*I'll be there for you* whenever you need someone*." as they could also be there for you when you need someone. *Love's the only rule* and *you really got me now* for *these arms are open all night* for you." and then he got up, turned, looked at me with his blue eyes, gave me the most amazing smile for a male and moved to another carriage.

The trip home didn't seem to take that long. I got off the train and exited the station and took a really good look around. Gee, I feel like a *stranger in this town*, even though I live here and *I love this town*.

I now know *these days*, that *it's my life*, not someone else's life, but mine to live, and that I should try to *have a nice day* everyday.

Upon *awakening* from my unusual dreams, I gave *April* a startling look and she said "Hey, *it's just me* your *Jersey girl*."

I thought "It's *all over now*." and I tried to tell her about my dreams but all she said was "*Shut up and kiss me* for *in these arms* you will find that I'll *always* be *in it for love*."

Then I heard that question "But WHO WILL SAVE NEW JERSEY?"

ANSWERS

It's *a brand new day in New Jersey* and I am back to a *real life,* the real world where a *miracle* could happen and usually does but *only in my dreams* for me.

"Last night my dreams seemed to come true as *you had me from hello* and then I was *kissed by an angel,* by you." I told April.

Then I told her about my dream: how I met a man dressed in *rawhide,* a dragon that wasn't a *wild thing,* not very nice heroes and I saw a *shooting star* through some *purple rain.* I also told her about the Queen and how she warned me to get ready because *we're having a party* tonight and that we would be singing *Happy Birthday Alec,* Simon, Peter, Sally and the *runaway.*

April told me "It was not really a dream but just you *goin' back* to your past to sort it out and to build a *bridge over troubled water.* You know that *I'll be there for you* always because *no one does it like you* and that's why *you keep me hanging on* to what we've got. I want you to *lay your hands on me* everyday that we're together.

You could have been like the *runaway* and missed the *homebound train* to stay and party all year long."

I said "*I am who I am* a Big Green Freak and *I haven't changed.*"

April replied softly "Not on the outside, no, but on the inside, yes.

You had to *break out* from your old ways and old ways of thinking to *get ready* for the next stage of your life. The dream and your experiences in it made you *open your heart* to the world and to the people in it. *If that's what it takes,* then that's *all that really matters.* Don't let anyone *steal your rock and roll* because that's what makes a part of you, who you are. Never will *you give love a bad name* because your heart will not let you. You may be a big green freak but I don't see you that way for I feel the tenderness and the love inside you when you *lay your hands on me.*

There are so many people in this world who are so different and who are made to feel unworthy because other people make judgements instantly by the way a person looks or acts and they never take the time to know the true person inside who could be the complete opposite to how the other people think they are.

Sometimes other people's judgements can cause insecurities to a person and that may be a cause for them not accepting their good points and causes the feeling that they are not worthy of being known and loved; but they are worthy of both.

You have been given the chance to meet people and hear their stories but you haven't judged them by what you have seen or heard and they haven't judged you in return by just looking at you and listening to you."

I thought "*I got me a woman* but *she don't know me*, but maybe I'm wrong because she does know me. *It's my life* and *the power* of *the music of my soul* will let me *have a nice day* every day."

She took my hand as we left to come here to the Oprah Show."

Oprah asked "Do you know why these dreams happened or do you blame someone for you having them?"

I said "Yes *blame it on the love of rock and roll,* you can't have *too much of a good thing*. It does *make me stronger*. You know that *the boys are back in town,* that fabulous *American Band,* the *Travelling Band...*"

Oprah interrupted me and asked "This question that you keep hearing, WHO WILL SAVE NEW JERSEY?

Well... do you know *THE ANSWER?"*

"Yes I do." I said "Why, who else but

JON
RICHIE
DAVID
TICO
HUEY
(and ALEC)

THE BOYS FROM BON JOVI

They will always be around to save New Jersey."

THE BON JOVI ALBUM SONGS, BON JOVI BOX SET SONGS AND THE CROSS ROADS 3 DISC SET STORY SECTION

THE BON JOVI ALBUM'S SONGS

My story starts from when the *King of the mountain* was amongst the prisoners in *the breakout* from the *Dry County* jail. He was accused of stealing a *diamond ring* from a *runaway* who was also *wanted dead or alive* because she was *wild in the streets* and *living in sin*.

The Sheriff and his Deputies chased some of the escapees down *Tokyo Road* until they reached the railway lines where some of the escapees boarded the *Homebound train,* others fled in *fast cars* along the *Lost Highway* while a couple of them took off on horses and as they rode away, they heard someone shout *"Ride cowboy ride."* The rest of the escapees split up when they reached the town of *Neurotica* which was a *two story town*.

The King and his cell mate stayed in the town for a few hours because it was *99 in the shade* in the *summertime* and they played *roulette,* drank *Bitter Wine* in the hotel and smoked their *last cigarette*.

The *runaway,* who was in the town, saw the escapees and notified the Sheriff but she was not caught herself. The Deputies arrived and found the escapees sleeping on a *bed of roses* out the back and shouted *"Raise your hands."*

They both tried to run but the King's cell mate was *shot through the heart* and the King was badly wounded and was taken to the County Hospital.

The doctors wanted to operate to remove the *bullet* in his side but he said "Don't you *lay your hands on me.* Just give me *something for the pain. Hook me up* to some *Novocaine;* you know that *bad medicine* that you give people."

The doctor said "If we don't operate on you now, you will die."

The King replied *"It's my life* and if I'm *living on a prayer* so be it. *Hey God,* I will *keep the faith* but I wanted to die in a *blaze of glory,* not like this; even though I know that I'm *wanted dead or alive."*

The King's wife Macy and his daughter Clare were brought to the hospital and when reunited with his family, he told his wife "The *story of my life* is *complicated* and that I have always been *in and out of love* because of a *dirty little secret* made *one wild night* many years ago.

48

I want you in these arms and *I want to be loved* for *without love* you're damned. *I don't wanna fall to the fire* but I need *something to believe in* not a *broken promise land.*"

The King then turned to his daughter and said "*You were born to be my baby* and *you had me from hello,* the first words I said to you when you were born. I thought I was *unbreakable* but *wild is the wind* and I ended up on the *right side of wrong* and being *wanted dead or alive.*

Don't *you give love a bad name* or become a *wildflower* or you'll always be *in and out of love. This ain't a love song* baby so *keep the faith,* have a *little bit of soul* and don't go *livin' on a prayer. Stick to your guns* and you'll never be *misunderstood. If I was your mother* I would help you *save the world* so that over the *next 100 years* you would still have a *bed of roses* to sleep on.

We weren't born to follow so *live before you die* but if you *learn to love* yourself and others, you will always hear the *bells of freedom* ringing for you."

Hey doc, I need some more *bad medicine in these arms* because I feel as if I have a *thorn in my side.* Then with more *blood on blood* on the bed, he looked back at his wife and quietly said "*Thank you for loving me.*" closed his eyes and died.

At the funeral *Captain Crash and the Beauty Queen from Mars* told the King's daughter that *I'll be there for you whenever* you need me and to *keep the faith.*

They then spoke to his sister in law Macy, the King's wife, and said "*She don't know me* and on *any other day* I would sit down and talk to her *till we ain't strangers anymore.* It would be *one step closer* for me to becoming her uncle again.

Everyday we get *just older* and sometimes *lonely;* however, *everybody's broken* at times and we have to learn how to *bounce* back and *have a nice day* and that could be hard for her to do as she is so young."

Then he said "Back in the days *when we were beautiful, we got it going on* by *rockin' in the free world. I love this town* still so *get ready* and *let it rock* again before a *whole lot of leaving* starts to happen once more."

That night, that *silent night,* Macy had her *secret dreams* again. In them her husband would *come back* to her *burning for love,* for he knew that she would say to him "*These arms are open all night* for you."

He would tell her in a soft voice "*Someday I'll be Saturday night* and *I'll be there for you. I'd die for you* so *never say goodbye.* I will *always run to you* because I love you but I find that *it's hard letting you go.* Don't ever think that *you give love a bad name* because when you *lay your hands on me* it's like *livin' on a prayer* that's been answered."

Then her dream vision changed to when she was a little girl and she was telling her mother "*My guitar lies bleeding in my arms* because I accidentally dropped it."

The following morning Clare went to work in a restaurant that is *open all night.* She would *work for the working man* giving him her *undivided* attention and service with a smile.

Miss Fourth of July often came into the restaurant.

"*She's a mystery.*" said a customer when he saw Miss July "because she catches the *Mystery Train* and will sit in the *seat next to you* if you are on it. *The distance* she travels *everyday* is not that far; however, she will either say to you in the morning "*Welcome to wherever you are.*" or in the afternoon "*Who says you can't go home?*"

After coming into the restaurant the following morning *Joey* said "*I don't like Mondays.* Last night I was with a *woman in love* but she only had her *love for sale* because she was *only lonely* and *the price of love* is just *hearts breaking even.* I know a few women and they *lie to me* by saying "*I'll be there for you,* but they never are, and *keep the faith.* But in who or what?"

Then he turned and said to Clare that he wanted to be her *superman tonight* and then asked her "Do *you want to make a memory?*"

He continued saying "*Everyday love lies* to me and I need *something to believe in. It's my life* and I would love for you to *lay your hands on me* and give me some of your *bad medicine* which would be *something for the pain* and to *love me back to life.*"

JOEY! You give love a bad name because love is not a *social disease.*

Remember it was you who told me that *one wild night* "*I got the girl*" and it was like *livin' on a prayer.*

If you were the *last man standing,* I would *runaway* from you because it's not *all about loving you.* Don't *say it isn't so* and I don't think *I could make a living out of loving you* ever. Before *the last night* I saw you, I didn't know if you were *wanted dead or alive* by some of the women you know but now to me it seems that all they really want to do is avoid you."

Clare then said *"These days,* I am *just older* and *fear* that *I get a rush* in knowing that *someday I'll be Saturday night.* I was starting to feel down about an hour ago so I decided to listen to some music and the *radio saved my life tonight* when I heard it playing the song *Always You Give Love A Bad Name.*

Did you know that on any day, the *hardest part is the night* to get through on your own? I don't want to take any *bad medicine* or be *in and out of love* and *I believe* that *it's my life* and that *love's the only rule* and *always* will be. You should *never say goodbye* to those you love for they need you as much as you need them even if you don't think you do."

In conclusion; the love from other people and from deep within yourself is all that you need and *if that's what it takes* for you to be *happy now,* then grab it by both hands and don't let it go. As for me, I will *blame it on the love of rock and roll* for I know that *I'll sleep when I'm dead* beneath a *bed of roses.*

I just love music as well as JON, RICHIE, DAVID, TICO and HUGH (and ALEC) from the greatest band BON JOVI... THANKS GUYS.

*   *   *   *   *

Every song from the following CDS has been used. (179 songs)
Bon Jovi
7800deg Fahrenheit
Slippery When Wet
New Jersey
Keep The Faith
Cross Roads
These Days
One Wild Night
Have A Nice Day
Bounce
This Left Feels Right
Crush
Lost Highway

The Circle

The BOX SET was not included as a different story using those songs has
been written.

*   *   *   *   *

BON JOVI BOX SET SONGS

In part of his *letter to a friend* the *rich man living in a poor man's
house* said "*Love ain't nothing but a four letter word* because *ordinary
people* are still *lonely at the top* even though they have *crazy love* and *too
much of a good thing.*

The *good guys don't always wear white* because the *outlaws of love* just
tried to *kidnap an angel* near *Garageland.* She was *the one that got away*
from the *edge of a broken heart.* They said that even though *we rule the
night,* she is the *thief of hearts* and is *out of bounds* to everyone except
her boyfriend *Satellite.*"

Recently I was talking to *Miss Fourth of July* who said that "*Someday
I'll be Saturday night* but until then *you can sleep while I dream* for *only
in my dreams, all I wanna do is you* to *shut up and kiss me.* I would
believe that *love ain't nothing but a four letter word* except *the fire inside
my flesh and bone* makes *every beat of my heart* want to tell you that
these arms are open all night for you if you need them. *I get a rush* just
thinking that *someday might just be tonight* when you say to me "*I just
want to be your man.*"

I over heard *Billy* talking to Miss July and he asked "*Why aren't you
dead?*"

Miss July replied "The *radio saved my life tonight* because I heard that
song "*Always Nobody's Hero*" by the band *Sympathy* and the *Last Man
Standing.*

That made me think that in *real life, maybe someday, starting all over
again* will mean catching the *last chance train,* and *taking it back* to
Memphis because *it's open all night* and *Memphis lives in me* and always
will be because that's where I was born and raised.

You *gotta have a reason* not to *breathe* but *if I can't have your love*
then the *temptation* will be, not to keep swimming until the *river runs
dry.*"

52

He told his friend that he was thankful for *JON, RICHIE, DAVID* and *TICO* (and *HUGH* and *ALEC*) for making this story possible and for writing great songs.

*   *   *   *   *

1,000,000 FANS CAN'T BE WRONG BOX SET

DISC 1

WHY AREN'T YOU DEAD

THE RADIO SAVED MY LIFE TONIGHT

TAKING IT BACK

SOMEDAY I'LL BE SATURDAY NIGHT

MISS FOURTH OF JULY

OPEN ALL NIGHT

THESE ARMS ARE OPEN ALL NIGHT

I GET A RUSH

SOMEDAY MIGHT JUST BE TONIGHT

THIEF OF HEARTS

LAST MAN STANDING

I JUST WANT TO BE YOUR MAN

DISC 2

GARAGELAND

STARTING ALL OVER AGAIN

MAYBE SOMEDAY

LAST CHANCE TRAIN

THE FIRE INSIDE

EVERY BEAT OF MY HEART

RICH MAN LIVING IN A POOR MAN'S HOUSE

THE ONE THAT GOT AWAY

YOU CAN SLEEP WHILE I DREAM

OUTLAWS OF LOVE

GOOD GUYS DON'T ALWAYS WEAR WHITE

WE RULE THE NIGHT

DISC 3

EDGE OF A BROKEN HEART

SYMPATHY

ONLY IN MY DREAMS

SHUT UP AND KISS ME

CRAZY LOVE

LONELY AT THE TOP

ORDINARY PEOPLE

FLESH AND BONE

SATELLITE

IF I CAN'T HAVE YOUR LOVE

REAL LIFE
MEMPHIS LIVES IN ME
TOO MUCH OF A GOOD THING
DISC 4
LOVE AIN'T NOTHING BUT A FOUR LETTER WORD
LOVE AIN'T NOTHING BUT A FOUR LETTER WORD
RIVER RUNS DRY
ALWAYS
KIDNAP AN ANGEL
BREATHE
OUT OF BOUNDS
LETTER TO A FRIEND
TEMPTATION
GOTTA HAVE A REASON
ALL I WANNA DO IS YOU
BILLY
NOBODY'S HERO
DISC 5 NOT INCLUDED IN THE STORY

*　　*　　*　　*　　*

CROSS ROADS 3 DISC SET

"*The boys are back in town* and are *wild in the streets* even though they are *wanted dead or alive* for stealing *Blood Money* from the bank. They are *livin' on a prayer* if the they think that they can leave in a *blaze of glory* after being *in and out of love*. There will *always* be *blood on blood* if a fight breaks out and you are shot twice in the head but you are still walking around." said the radio announcer.

"Hang on! If you are shot twice in the head, then *why aren't you dead?" Lucky* asked.

The *runaway* replied "You have to *keep the faith* that *I'll be there for you* even if *you give love a bad name,* especially as *good guys don't always wear white.* It's like when you received that *postcard from the Wasteland* which is on the *edge of a broken heart.*

On the back it read "The *radio saved my life tonight* after I heard that for *starting all over again,* you have to *save a prayer, raise your hands* and *let it rock. Someday I'll be Saturday night* because *in these arms* you can give me some *bad medicine* while we lay on a *bed of roses.* You can *lay your hands on me* and I will give you this *diamond ring* and will

54

promise to *never say goodbye*." and the signature was smudged so you don't know who sent it to you.

As for being shot twice in the head; it would be where the bullets planted themselves as to whether they would kill you or not."

*   *   *   *   *

CROSS ROADS (3 DISC SET)
DISC 1
LIVIN' ON A PRAYER
KEEP THE FAITH
SOMEDAY I'LL BE SATURDAY NIGHT
ALWAYS
WANTED DEAD OR ALIVE
LAY YOUR HANDS ON ME
YOU GIVE LOVE A BAD NAME
BED OF ROSES
BLAZE OF GLORY
IN THESE ARMS
BAD MEDICINE
I'LL BE THERE FOR YOU
IN AND OUT OF LOVE
RUNAWAY
NEVER SAY GOODBYE
DISC 2
RADIO SAVED MY LIFE TONIGHT
WILD IN THE STREETS
DIAMOND RING
GOOD GUYS DON'T ALWAYS WEAR WHITE
THE BOYS ARE BACK IN TOWN
EDGE OF A BROKEN HEART
POSTCARD FROM THE WASTELAND
BLOOD ON BLOOD
LET IT ROCK
STARTING ALL OVER AGAIN
BLOOD MONEY
SAVE A PRAYER
LUCKY
WHY AREN'T YOU DEAD
RAISE YOUR HANDS

DISC 3
LIVIN' ON A PRAYER
YOU GIVE LOVE A BAD NAME
KEEP THE FAITH
ALWAYS
BLAZE OF GLORY
I'LL SLEEP WHEN I'M DEAD
PAPA WAS A ROLLING STONE
BAD MEDICINE
SHOUT
HEY GOD
WANTED DEAD OR ALIVE
THIS AIN'T A LOVE SONG
THESE DAYS

WANTED
DEAD OR ALIVE

JON BON JOVI - JON BONGIOVI

For having the knack for writing,
recording and performing great songs
whether it be live performances, in
concerts recorded on video or DVD or
on a CD. Your talent has grown since
the Power Station Years and I have
included those songs in this book.

JON BON JOVI SONG

I used the Songs from the albums Destination Anywhere, Blaze of Glory and the Christmas Single to write the following.

On *August 7, 4.15* in a *little city* named *Guano City,* a battle erupted over *Blood Money*. There went *justice in the barrel* of many guns especially after the *back door frenzy* broke out.

"You know that *learning how to fall* is essential because *dyin' ain't much of a livin'* so *never say die*. *Billy get your guns* and ride to *Santa Fe* for help, but be careful that you don't get shot through your *cold hard heart*. You know that they'll never *bang a drum* for you at *midnight in Chelsea* if you try to go out in a *blaze of glory* and you will be buried *naked* and *ugly*." said the *Queen of New Orleans*.

Then she said "Please tell your sister; *Janie, don't take your love to town* and *please come home for Christmas*. You *really got me now* thinking that *every word was a piece of my heart* when I said them and *I wish everyday could be like Christmas*. I also remember you telling me that " *it's just me staring at your window with a suitcase in my hands* heading for a *destination anywhere* and it would not take a *miracle* for me to stay and not go back home."

*   *   *   *   *

THE POWER STATION YEARS STORY

Whilst walking through an unusual building, Adrian saw the *runaway*. He knew that *this woman is dangerous* but he had to find out if she was *Bobby's girl*.

He approached her and they started talking, then she said "It's too open to talk here. Come let's go into that room over there."

They went into a medium sized room that was furnished with a lounge setting, so they sat down.

Adrian: "Bobby said that you were his girlfriend and I want to know if that was true."
                "Bobby said that you were his girlfriend and I want to know if that was true."

Runaway: "*Don't you believe him* because he lives in his *Hollywood dreams* and is always *stringin' a line* to me."
                "*Don't you believe him* because he lives in his *Hollywood*

58

dreams and is always *stringin' a line* to me."

Adrian: "Are you saying that he is *all talk, no action?*"
"Are you saying that he is *all talk, no action?*"

Runaway: "Yes. *We get more than we bargained for* when we get to know someone and anyway *who said it would last forever?*"
"Yes. *We get more than we bargained for* when we get to know someone and anyway *who said it would last forever?*"

They paused in their conversation for a moment and looked at each other with a puzzling expression on their faces.

Runaway: "Has anyone heard you *talkin' in your sleep?*"
"Has anyone heard you *talkin' in your sleep?*"

Adrian: "No. Why. What do you want to know for*?*"
"No. Why. What do you want to know for*?*"

Runaway: "Please *don't keep me wondering* whether you could *open your heart* and love me because I'm *head over heels* in love with you."
"Please *don't keep me wondering* whether you could *open your heart* and love me because I'm *head over heels* in love with you."

Adrian: "*For you* I think I can because *no one does it like you.*"
"*For you* I think I can because *no one does it like you.*"

Runaway: "*Don't leave me tonight.*"
"*Don't leave me tonight.*"

Then she paused again and looked at Adrian. She motioned with her finger for him to be quiet, then took his hand and left the room.

Adrian: "What's all that about?"

Runaway: "That room. I think that we were talking in an echo chamber".

Adrian: "*Maybe tomorrow* you can *gimme some lovin' Charlene.* Yes, I know who you really are, so *don't do that to me anymore* by pretending you are somebody else."

*   *   *   *   *

59

ALL JON BON JOVI SONGS STORY

As I stood *standing at your window with a suitcase in my hand,* I remembered when you were *talkin' in your sleep* and you said *"Who said it would last forever* because *dyin' ain't that much of a livin'.* I was just *stringin' a line* to you about me being *head over heels* in love with you."

I thought "I'm in one of those *Hollywood dreams* where the words from your *cold hard heart* became the *justice in the barrel* of your gun. I am going to leave *Santa Fe* and catch the train on *August 7, 4.15,* maybe to *Guano City* or a *destination anywhere* as long as it is far away from you. I guess that we got *more than we bargained for* and you ended up being *all talk, no action. Don't keep me wondering* if you could *open your heart* and *gimme some lovin' Charlene.*"

After I reached the station and while waiting for the train I heard another man begging *"Janie, don't take your love to town.* Please *don't leave me tonight.* You know that for me *no one does it like you* and please *don't you believe him* when he says that I was with another woman at *midnight in Chelsea.* It wasn't me because I was visiting my mother, the *Queen of New Orleans* at that time."

Then she said "I don't care if you *bang a drum,* stand *naked* in the street or *runaway. For you,* I would say *Billy get your guns* and shoot him before the sun rises in a *blaze of glory* for the *blood money* I would pay him, just to get rid of you."

The man said "Janie, *What do you want?"*

Janie said "I want to be *Bobby's girl* because he is not *all talk, no action* like you are. He doesn't live in his *Hollywood dreams* and besides he's not *ugly* like you are."

I thought "Gee, I think *this woman is dangerous.*" After hearing what she said, I don't think that I want to start *learning how to fall* out of love with my beautiful wife Charlene.

I left the station and went home.

As I walked through the door I said *"It's just me.* Can we sit and talk please."

Charlene said "As long as you're not *stringin' a line* to me and please *don't keep me wondering* why you left."

I said "I heard you *talkin' in your sleep* and thought that it was me you were talking to. I didn't take the time to find out the truth. I am still *head over heels* in love with you and when we took our vows *every word was a piece of my heart* at the time and they still are. *No one does it like you* and *you really got me now*. Please *open your heart* and forgive me."

Charlene looked at me and said "*Don't do that to me anymore*. I wasn't talking to you at all; I must have been rehearsing my lines for my play in my sleep. *Maybe tomorrow* you can help me go through some of them."

I asked "Would you like to go through some of them now?"

Charlene handed me a couple of sheets of paper and said "You are Jimmy and I am Sandra and we are in a three way conversation. You speak first."

Jimmy: "*What do you want?*"

Sandra: "*Don't leave me tonight.*"

Jimmy: "And *who says it would last forever?*"

Sandra: "But we may get *more than we bargained for.*"

Jimmy: "*Don't you believe him?*"

Sandra   "*For you* I'll *never say die.*"

I said "I think that you will be great in the play and I am so glad that I came back because I could have ruined both our lives for being so stupid.

What is the name of the play again?"

Charlene said "IT'S A *MIRACLE*."

*   *   *   *   *

REFERENCE

THE POWER STATION YEARS
WHO SAID IT WOULD LAST FOREVER
OPEN YOUR HEART
STRINGIN' A LINE
DON'T LEAVE ME TONIGHT

MORE THAN WE BARGAINED FOR
FOR YOU
HOLLYWOOD DREAMS
ALL TALK, NO ACTION
DON'T KEEP ME WONDERING
HEAD OVER HEELS
NO ONE DOES IT LIKE YOU
WHAT YOU WANT
DON'T YOU BELIEVE HIM
TALKIN' IN YOUR SLEEP

MORE POWER STATION YEARS
WHO SAID IT WOULD LAST FOREVER
OPEN YOUR HEART
STRINGIN' A LINE
DON'T LEAVE ME TONIGHT
MORE THAN WE BARGAINED FOR
FOR YOU
HOLLYWOOD DREAMS
ALL TALK, NO ACTION
DON'T KEEP ME WONDERING
HEAD OVER HEELS
NO ONE DOES IT LIKE YOU
WHAT YOU WANT
DON'T YOU BELIEVE HIM
TALKIN' IN YOUR SLEEP
BOBBY'S GIRL
GIMME SOME LOVIN' CHARLENE
DON'T DO THAT TO ME ANYMORE
THIS WOMAN IS DANGEROUS
MAYBE TOMORROW
RUNAWAY

BLAZE OF GLORY
BILLY GET YOUR GUNS
MIRACLE
BLAZE OF GLORY
BLOOD MONEY
SANTA FE
JUSTICE IN THE BARREL
NEVER SAY DIE
YOU REALLY GOT ME NOW
BANG A DRUM
DYIN' AIN'T MUCH OF A LIVIN'

GUANO CITY

DESTINATION ANYWHERE
QUEEN OF NEW ORLEANS
JANIE, DON'T TAKE YOUR LOVE TO TOWN
MIDNIGHT IN CHELSEA
UGLY
STARING AT YOUR WINDOW WITH A SUITCASE IN MY HAND
EVERY WORD WAS A PIECE OF MY HEART
IT'S JUST ME
DESTINATION ANYWHERE
LEARNING HOW TO FALL
NAKED
LIITLE CITY
AUGUST 7, 4.15
COLD HARD HEART

BON JOVI CHRISTMAS
PLEASE COME HOME FOR CHRISTMAS
I WISH EVERYDAY COULD BE LIKE CHRISTMAS
BACK DOOR FRENZY

WANTED
DEAD OR ALIVE

RICHIE SAMBORA

For having the knack for writing, recording and performing great songs whether it be live performances, in concert recorded on video or DVD or on a CD. Your talent as a solo artist is also shown through your solo albums They are also included in this book

RICHIE SAMBORA'S SONGS

After *Mr. Bluesman* sang his *Ballad of Youth* in the *Harlem rain*, he said that he was *made in America* although he was a *stranger in this town* and when he arrived, he only saw *one light burning* beside the *River of Love*.

He said that "*Who I am* is *all that really matters* because *hard times come easy* when you're *chained* to the *downside of love* and you have *fallen from Graceland*. Know this *Rosie*, I am *in it for love* but *if I can't have your love* I will go to the *Church of Desire* and try to *rest in peace* until I can find love again. I also know that *if God was a woman* she would say that *you're not alone* and to ask *Father Time* for *the answer* to finding my *undiscovered soul*."

*   *   *   *   *

SHARK FRENZY ONE & TWO

In the *Confessions of a Teenage Lycanthrope* it was revealed that *come Saturday night* the *law of the jungle* is that *nobody* can stop a *devil on the run* except the *man with a dragon* or *the ones with the angel eyes*. The *Platinum Heroes* thought that they had *the power* to stop him, *till the walls come down* on the *cruising lines* and *the crashing kites out in the heat*.

It was also revealed that he had, had a *good life* up until his last *birthday* when he accidentally let slip his undisclosed condition to his girlfriend *Southern Belle*.

He pleaded with her "Please *don't leave me now, I need your love* to get me through. There isn't *any other woman like you* that *I'll play the fool* for."

Belle replied "*Fool, fool, fool, I haven't changed* for you to *live fast, love hard, die young* in *golden slumber*. You only think I have."

*   *   *   *   *

ALL RICHIE SAMBORA'S SONGS

"*If God was a woman*." said *Father Time* from the pulpit in the *Church of Desire* "*Nobody* would *rest in peace* with the *devil on the run*. He has *fallen from Graceland* and *the ones with the angel eyes* are trying to catch him. If they can't then your *undiscovered soul* could become *chained* to the *downside of love.*"

Then there was a silence as Father Time looked around the small congregation.

"Remember *you're not alone* and if you are *a stranger in this town, the power* of love will help you to live a *good life.* To *live fast, love hard, die young* is not *the answer.*

The *law of the jungle* states that although *hard times come easy* once you've been down for awhile, the only way to start going is up. Keeping the family together is *all that really matters* so you all have to stick together *till the walls come down* and be *in it for love.*

This is the end of the sermon for today. I will be taking confessions in half an hour for those who need to attend. We will close the service by singing the Vespers."

There were a few people waiting for confession when Father Time entered the church. He heard the *Confessions of a Teenage Lycanthrope* first and then the *Platinum Heroes;* all seven of them but one at a time.

After the service a few families went for a picnic in a park nearby. Five children played *out in the heat,* four children had *the crashing kites* and one child said to another child "*Fool, fool, fool,* you need to get your mother to buy you a kite like mine. It's *made in America* and the *cruising lines* don't get tangled up. If you *don't leave me now,* I will let you fly it for awhile."

Mr. Bluesman headed off down the road because he had to attend a *birthday* party. He was going to play the *Ballad of Youth* and a few other songs if the *Harlem rain* didn't start coming down. He told the guests that he would play just about anything but *I'll play the fool* for nobody.

The *Southern Belle* was walking with *Rosie* to her place when she excitedly said "Rosie, *come Saturday night* I will be on my holiday at the *Golden Slumber Retreat.* I wish you could have come too."

Rosie said that the commitment she already had, couldn't be cancelled.

Little did the Southern Belle know that Rosie had a secret rendezvous with the *man with a dragon,* whom she was meeting on the grassy banks of the *River of Love.*

There was *one light burning* near the place where they met that evening and the man said to Rosie "There isn't *any other woman like you* and *if I can't have your love* then I don't know what I'll do. *I need your love* and *I am who I am, I haven't changed.*"

Rosie said "OK what have you been up to? What are you feeling guilty about? I should know you by now and when something's up 'cos we've been married for twenty years."

*   *   *   *   *

REFERENCE

SHARK FRENZY ONE
COME SATURDAY NIGHT
LIVE FAST, LOVE HARD, DIE YOUNG
LAW OF THE JUNGLE
NOBODY
THE ONES WITH THE ANGEL EYES
THE POWER
I'LL PLAY THE FOOL
BIRTHDAY
DON'T STOP LOVING ME NOW
SOUTHERN BELLE
PLATINUM HEROES

SHARK FRENZY TWO
CONFESSIONS OF A TEENAGE LYCANTHORPE
A GOOD LIFE
I HAVEN'T CHANGED
CRUISING LINES
ANY WOMAN LIKE YOU
I NEED YOUR LOVE
DEVIL ON THE RUN
MAN WITH A DRAGON
CRASHING KITES
TILL THE WALLS COME DOWN
FOOL, FOOL, FOOL
OUT IN THE HEAT
GOLDEN SLUMBER

STRANGER IN THIS TOWN
REST IN PEACE
CHURCH OF DESIRE

STRANGER IN THIS TOWN
BALLAD OF YOUTH
ONE LIGHT BURNING
MR BLUESMAN
ROSIE
RIVER OF LOVE
FATHER TIME
THE ANSWER

UNDISCOVERED SOUL
MADE IN AMERICA
HARD TIMES COME EASY
FALLEN FROM GRACELANDS
IF GOD WAS A WOMAN
ALL THAT REALLY MATTERS
YOU'RE NOT ALONE
IN IT FOR LOVE
CHAINED
HARLEM RAIN
WHO I AM
DOWNSIDE OF LOVE
UNDISCOVERED SOUL

WANTED
DEAD OR ALIVE

DAVID BRYAN

For having the knack for writing, recording and performing great songs whether it be live performances, in concerts recorded on video or DVD or on a CD. Your brilliance and talent as a solo artist is shown through your solo albums and your musical shows that have also been used in this book.

DAVID BRYAN'S SONGS

It's a long road back to Memphis where *in these arms* I was *kissed by an angel* while dancing the *Netherworld Waltz* with you. But that night *on a full moon, the midnight voodoo* hit me when *you tore my heart out* as in the *Interlude* you left and went *up the river* with *April,* leaving me in a *room full of blues.*

It was an *awakening* but on the *endless horizon* of my *summer of dreams,* I had a *second chance* because I knew that *I can love. This time* I will sing a *Lullaby for Two Moons* and ask the Lord to *hear our prayer* as we pray for forgiveness, peace and strength to carry on and love again. I know that I will because I am back home in Memphis and that *Memphis lives in me* and always will.

Thank you David, for writing such beautiful songs that I hope that one day you will play and sing them on a DVD for all your fans. I have taken the songs from both On A Full Moon and Lunar Eclipse but only used the song titles once.

*   *   *   *   *

DAVID BRYAN'S MUSICAL SONGS

The Legend of the Toxic Avenger was started *underground* by a *colored woman* who went *into the Netherworld* to get away from *a brand new day in New Jersey.*

She told another person that *"Everybody wants to be black on Saturday night* because the *radio* will be playing my kind of music all along the *Black Magic River. Someday the music of my soul* will want me to *say a prayer* to *make me stronger* and for me to be able to *stand up* against *my father's sins.* Although *everybody dies* at some time, just remember you don't *inherit the dead.*

However you might just find that *evil is hot* in some places where you might visit whilst you are still alive."

The other person replied "You must be careful in some places because *the birds of a feather* will stick together when they come to *steal your rock and roll* and take it to the *bitch/slut /liar/ whore* at *Tonk's place.*

Now that's a place, where you will find an *open door policy* for *hot toxic love* between a *stranger to love* and a *big green geek* or just about anyone.

So *"What's your pleasure?"* You will be asked by someone from across the way."

The first woman said "Yes, I know and you may also hear the *Jersey girl* saying *"My big French boyfriend* will *get the geek* and *kick your ass* if *you tore my heart out. All men are freaks ."*

Pointing to the female walking into the open room, the Jersey girl said *"Thank God she's blind* so she can't see me *scratch my itch* on my backside when it gets bad."

Were you there when a man entered the room and said *"Hello, my name is Huey* and I've come to tell you that *love will stand when all else falls* and *change don't come easy* especially when you think *big love ain't nothing but a kiss.* You know that *you tore my heart out* last night but *if I didn't love you,* I would *tear down the house* and move back to Memphis because *Memphis lives in me."* said the second person.

"I was there." said a third person "when *crazy little Huey* added that at *the ceremony* I will not give you *100 reasons* for not dancing the *Netherworld Waltz* with Jersey girl, but one; *she's my sister* and a *mirror image* of our mother, the colored woman."

The conversation was interrupted when they all heard "But *Who will save New Jersey?"* the question being asked repeatedly on the television in the background.

Choose me, Oprah! came a voice out of nowhere".

*   *   *   *   *

ALL DAVID BRYAN' S SONGS

In my *summer of dreams* I want to go and visit the guys *who will save New Jersey.* I know that *it's a long road into the Netherworld* to get to *Tonk's place.*

Once I get there I know that *everybody wants to be black on Saturday night* so they can also get into the *Interlude* Club to listen to the band *Birds of a Feather* fill a *room full of blues* by playing a *Lullaby for Two Moons.* In this club; sometimes *on a full moon,* someone will be *kissed by an angel* and will either be taken *up the river* or they will dance the *Netherworld Waltz* with them.

71

If you are taken *up the river,* you had better *say a prayer* because *evil is hot* up there and you may *inherit the dead* or *my father's sins* or find that love *ain't nothing but a kiss.* No matter what happens, it will be an *awakening* for you especially when you see the *endless horizon* of faces that are a *mirror image* of your own.

One woman who was taken there came back a *bitch/slut/liar/whore* and a *stranger to love.* The club's owner was shocked and asked everyone to *stand up* and he asked the Lord to *hear our prayer* as we pray for her soul and to *thank God she's blind* so she couldn't see that *all men are freaks* in their own way.

To leave the *Interlude* Club or Tonk's place, you have to go *underground* and travel north through the Heartlands.

Whilst travelling, you may hear about the *Legend of the Toxic Avenger* who is a *big green freak.* They say that he will try to take your *radio* so he can *steal your rock and roll.*

"*Everybody dies,* except me" he will say "and as *Memphis lives in me* and since *you tore my heart out,* I think that I will *kick your ass* and not give you any *hot toxic love* candy.

Watch out for *April* 'cos *she's my sister* but she is different from me. If she was here now, she would *scratch my itch* and give me *big love.* I would take her *in these arms,* sing her a *Lullaby for Two Moons* and dance the *Netherworld Waltz* with her because *love will stand when all else falls.*"

It's a long road through the Heartlands and all I see is an *endless horizon* of shimmering heat.

Suddenly I heard "*Hello, my name is Huey* although some people call me *crazy little Huey.* Are you looking for *April?*" said a man with a strange accent.

I turned around to see a man standing behind me and a woman approaching from behind him. "Don't mind him *he's my big French boyfriend* who wants to *get the geek* that's heading this way."

I said that I was just passing through and looking for a place to rest a while and maybe get something to eat and drink.

April asked "Have you come from the Interlude Club?"

72

I replied "Yes."

April said "You're lucky to get a *second chance* because not many people get out of there or past my brother who can also be a bit weird. You must have told him something that he liked for him to let you pass."

Then I said "You know it's funny, but *Memphis lives in me* as well and I think that there would be at least *100 reasons* for why it does."

Huey said "*Change don't come easy* to many people so let us pray and ask the Lord to *hear our prayer* to make you and *make me stronger* for the hard times to come."

April said "Just down the road you will come to a bridge that crosses the *Black Magic River* and on the other side is the *Midnight Voodoo* Hotel that is owned and run by a *colored woman*.

Tell her that April sent you and she will look after you. She has an *open door policy* and *this time* if you are lucky enough to get *kissed by an angel on a full moon,* nothing but good things will happen to you. I now have to go and sort Huey and my brother out and give them their medication."

Huey turned to April and said "*If I didn't love you* I would *tear down the house* if *you tore my heart out.*"

April shook her head bemused, turned and walked away with Huey following close behind.

I reached the hotel and the owner asked "*What's your pleasure?*"

I told her that April sent me and the smile that came across her face lit the room.

The owner then said "We are watching a new program called *The Ceremony* where someone in the audience says *Choose me! Oprah* and if you are chosen, you have to get up and dance the *Netherworld Waltz*. I'll tell you now; nobody will ever get *in these arms* that way. When the program's finished, we are going to fill this *room full of blues* because it is the *music of my soul.*"

"AHHH!! What a nightmare that was.

Someday my *summer of dreams* to meet the boys will come true but right now I know *I can love a brand new day in New Jersey.*" said the *Jersey girl.*

REFERENCE

ON A FULL MOON
AWAKENING
IT'S A LONG ROAD
ON A FULL MOON
APRIL
KISSED BY AN ANGEL
ENDLESS HORIZON
IN THESE ARMS
LULLABY FOR TWO MOONS
INTERLUDE
MIDNIGHT VOODOO
ROOM FULL OF BLUES
HEAR OUR PRAYER
SUMMER OF DREAMS
UP THE RIVER
NETHERWORLD WALTZ

LUNAR ECLIPSE
SECOND CHANCE
I CAN LOVE
IT'S A LONG ROAD
ON A FULL MOON
APRIL
KISSED BY AN ANGEL
ENDLESS HORIZON
LULLABY FOR TWO MOONS
INTERLUDE
ROOM FULL OF BLUES
HEAR OUR PRAYER
SUMMER OF DREAMS
UP THE RIVER
NETHERWORLD WALTZ
IN THESE ARMS

NETHERWORLD SOUNDTRACK
STRANGER TO LOVE
TONK'S PLACE
BIRDS OF A FEATHER
BLACK MAGIC RIVER
OPEN DOOR POLICY
MY FATHER'S SINS

THE CEREMONY
INTO THE NETHERWORLD
IF I DIDN'T LOVE YOU
INHERIT THE DEAD
MIRROR IMAGE
WHAT'S YOUR PLEASURE
100 REASONS
NETHERWORLD WALTZ

THE TOXIC AVENGER SOUNDTRACK
WHO WILL SAVE NEW JERSEY
JERSEY GIRL
GET THE GEEK
KICK YOUR ASS
MY BIG FRENCH BOYFRIEND
THANK GOD SHE'S BLIND
BIG GREEN FREAK
CHOOSE ME, OPRAH!
HOT TOXIC LOVE
THE LEGEND OF THE TOXIC AVENGER
EVIL IS HOT
BITCH/SLUT/LIAR/WHORE
EVERYBODY DIES
YOU TORE MY HEART OUT
ALL MEN ARE FREAKS
A BRAND NEW DAY IN NEW JERSEY
YOU TORE MY HEART OUT

MEMPHIS MUSICAL SOUNDTRACK
UNDERGROUND
THE MUSIC OF MY SOUL
SCRATCH MY ITCH
AIN'T NOTHIN' BUT A KISS
HELLO, MY NAME IS HUEY
EVERYBODY WANTS TO BE BLACK ON SATURDAY NIGHT
MAKE ME STRONGER
COLORED WOMAN
SOMEDAY
SHE'S MY SISTER
RADIO
SAY A PRAYER
CRAZY LITTLE HUEY
BIG LOVE

LOVE WILL STAND WHEN ALL ELSE FALLS
STAND UP
CHANGE DON'T COME EASY
TEAR THE HOUSE DOWN
LOVE WILL STAND WHEN ALL ELSE FALLS
AIN'T NOTHIN' BUT A KISS
MEMPHIS LIVES IN ME
STEAL YOUR ROCK AND ROLL

WANTED
DEAD OR ALIVE

TICO TORRES

For helping the rest of the band
during the recording and performing
of the great songs whether it be in live
performances, or in concert
recorded on video or DVD or
on a CD.

WANTED
DEAD OR ALIVE

HUGH MCDONALD

For helping the rest of the band
during the recording and performing
of the great songs whether it be in live
performances, or in concert
recorded on video or DVD or
on a CD.

WANTED
DEAD OR ALIVE

ALEC JOHN SUCH

For helping the rest of the band during the recording and performing of
the great songs whether it be in live
performances, or in concert recorded
on video or DVD or on a CD.

REFERENCE

THE BAND'S ALBUMS (CDs)

BON JOVI
RUNAWAY
ROULETTE
SHE DON'T KNOW ME
SHOT THROUGH THE HEART
LOVE LIES
BREAKOUT
BURNING FOR LOVE
COME BACK
GET READY

7800 deg FARENHEIT
IN AND OUT OF LOVE
THE PRICE OF LOVE
ONLY LONELY
KING OF THE MOUNTAIN
SILENT NIGHT
TOKYO ROAD
THE HARDEST PART OF THE NIGHT
ALWAYS RUN TO YOU
(I DON'T WANT TO) FALL TO THE FIRE
SECRET DREAMS
IN AND OUT OF LOVE

SLIPPERY WHEN WET
LET IT ROCK
YOU GIVE LOVE A BAD NAME
LIVIN' ON A PRAYER
SOCIAL DISEASE
WANTED DEAD OR ALIVE
RAISE YOUR HANDS
WITHOUT LOVE
I'D DIE FOR YOU
NEVER SAY GOODBYE
ILD IN THE STREETS
WANTED DEAD OR ALIVE

NEW JERSEY
LAY YOUR HANDS ON ME
BAD MEDICINE

BORN TO BE MY BABY
LIVING IN SIN
BLOOD ON BLOOD
HOMEBOUND TRAIN
WILD IS THE WIND
RIDE COWBOY RIDE
STICK TO YOUR GUNS
I'LL BE THERE FOR YOU
99 IN THE SHADE
LOVE FOR SALE
LAY YOUR HANDS ON ME

KEEP THE FAITH
I BELIEVE
KEEP THE FAITH
I'LL SLEEP WHEN I'M DEAD
IN THESE ARMS
BED OF ROSES
IF I WAS YOUR MOTHER
DRY COUNTY
WOMAN IN LOVE
FEAR
I WANT YOU
BLAME IT ON THE LOVE OF ROCK AND ROLL
LITTLE BIT OF SOUL
KEEP THE FAITH

CROSS ROADS
LIVIN' ON A PRAYER
KEEP THE FAITH
SOMEDAY I'LL BE SATURDAY NIGHT
ALWAYS
WANTED DEAD OR ALIVE
LAY YOUR HANDS ON ME
YOU GIVE LOVE A BAD NAME
BED OF ROSES
BLAZE OF GLORY
IN THESE ARMS
BAD MEDICINE
I'LL BE THERE FOR YOU
IN AND OUT OF LOVE
RUNAWAY
NEVER SAY GOODBYE

THESE DAYS
HEY GOD
SOMETHING FOR THE PAIN
THIS AIN'T A LOVE SONG
THESE DAYS
LIE TO ME
DAMNED
MY GUITAR LIES BLEEDING IN MY ARMS
(IT'S HARD) LETTING YOU GO
HEARTS BREAKING EVEN
SOMETHING TO BELIEVE IN
IF THAT'S WHAT IT TAKES
DIAMOND RING
BITTER WINE
THESE DAYS

THESE DAYS DOUBLE CD
FIRST CD
HEY GOD
SOMETHING FOR THE PAIN
THIS AIN'T A LOVE SONG
THESE DAYS
LIE TO ME
DAMNED
MY GUITAR LIES BLEEDING IN MY ARMS
IT'S HARD LETTING YOU GO
HEARTS BREAKING EVEN
SOMETHING TO BELIEVE IN
IF THAT'S WHAT IT TAKES
DIAMOND RING
ALL I WANT IS EVERY THING
BITTER WINE
SECOND CD
THIS AIN'T A LOVE SONG
I DON'T LIKE MONDAYS
LIVIN' ON A PRAYER
YOU GIVE LOVE A BAD NAME
WILD IN THE STREETS

ONE WILD NIGHT
IT'S MY LIFE
LIVIN' ON A PRAYER
YOU GIVE LOVE A BAD NAME
KEEP THE FAITH

SOMEDAY I'LL BE SATURDAY NIGHT
ROCKIN' IN THE FREE WORLD
SOMETHING TO BELIEVE IN
WANTED DEAD OR ALIVE
RUNAWAY
IN AND OUT OF LOVE
I DON'T LIKE MONDAYS
JUST OLDER
SOMETHING FOR THE PAIN
BAD MEDICINE
ONE WILD NIGHT

HAVE A NICE DAY DOUBLE CD (Australian Edition)
FIRST CD
HAVE A NICE DAY
I WANT TO BE LOVED
WELCOME TO WHEREVER YOU ARE
WHO SAYS YOU CAN'T GO HOME
LAST MAN STANDING
BELLS OF FREEDOM
WILDFLOWER
LAST CIGARETTE
COMPLICATED
NOVOCAINE
STORY OF MY LIFE
DIRTY LITTLE SECRET
UNBREAKABLE
SECOND CD
EVERYDAY
MISS FOURTH OF JULY
I GET A RUSH
THESE ARMS ARE OPEN ALL NIGHT
THE RADIO SAVED MY LIFE TONIGHT

BOUNCE
UNDIVIDED
EVERYDAY
THE DISTANCE
JOEY
MISUNDERSTOOD
ALL ABOUT LOVIN' YOU
HOOK ME UP
RIGHT SIDE OF WRONG
LOVE ME BACK TO LIFE

YOU HAD ME FROM HELLO
BOUNCE
OPEN ALL NIGHT

THIS LEFT FEELS RIGHT
WANTED DEAD OR ALIVE
LIVIN' ON A PRAYER
BAD MEDICINE
IT'S MY LIFE
LAY YOUR HANDS ON ME
YOU GIVE LOVE A BAD NAME
BED OF ROSES
EVERYDAY
BORN TO BE MY BABY
KEEP THE FAITH
I'LL BE THERE FOR YOU
ALWAYS

CRUSH
IT'S MY LIFE
SAY IT ISN'T SO
THANK YOU FOR LOVING ME
TWO STORY TOWN
NEXT 100 YEARS
JUST OLDER
MYSTERY TRAIN
SAVE THE WORLD
CAPTAIN CRASH AND THE BEAUTY QUEEN FROM MARS
SHE'S A MYSTERY
I GOT THE GIRL
ONE WILD NIGHT
I COULD MAKE A LIVING OUT OF LOVIN' YOU
NEUROTICA

LOST HIGHWAY SPECIAL AUSTRALIAN EDITION
LOST HIGHWAY
SUMMERTIME
YOU WANT TO MAKE A MEMORY
WHOLE LOT OF LEAVING
WE GOT IT GOING ON
ANY OTHER DAY
SEAT NEXT TO YOU
EVERYBODY'S BROKEN
TILL WE AIN'T STRANGERS ANYMORE

THE LAST NIGHT
ONE STEP CLOSER
I LOVE THIS TOWN
LONELY

THE CIRCLE
WE WEREN'T BORN TO FOLLOW
WHEN WE WERE BEAUTIFUL
WORK FOR THE WORKING MAN
SUPERMAN TONIGHT
BULLET
THORN IN MY SIDE
LIVE BEFORE YOU DIE
BROKEN PROMISE LAND
LOVE'S THE ONLY RULE
FAST CARS
HAPPY NOW
LEARN TO LOVE

THE BAND'S CONCERTS AND VIDEOS (NOT IN ORDER)

THE FORUM, MILAN, ITALY 1993
YOU GIVE LOVE A BAD NAME
CAN'T HELP FALLING IN LOVE
BED OF ROSES
KEEP THE FAITH
BLAZE OF GLORY
DRY COUNTY
WANTED DEAD OR ALIVE
IN THESE ARMS
WITH A LITTLE HELP FROM MY FRIENDS
LIVIN' ON A PRAYER
BAD MEDICINE

MULTI SHOWS BRAZIL 1997 – 2003
1997
LIVIN' ON A PRAYER
JANIE, DON'T TAKE YOUR LOVE TO TOWN
MIDNIGHT IN CHELSEA
DESTINATION ANYWHERE
BED OF ROSES
2003
BOUNCE

EVERYDAY
YOU GIVE LOVE A BAD NAME
MISUNDERSTOOD
IT'S MY LIFE
BOUNCE

LIVE FROM LONDON 1995
LIVIN' ON A PRAYER
YOU GIVE LOVE A BAD NAME
KEEP THE FAITH
ALWAYS
BLAZE OF GLORY
LAY YOUR HANDS ON ME
I'LL SLEEP WHEN I'M DEAD
PAPA WAS A ROLLING STONE
BAD MEDICINE
SHOUT
HEY GOD
WANTED DEAD OR ALIVE
THESE DAYS
THIS AIN'T A LOVE SONG

THE CRUSH TOUR
INTRO
LIVIN' ON A PRAYER
YOU GIVE LOVE A BAD NAME
CAPTAIN CRASH AND THE BEAUTY QUEEN FROM MARS
SAY IT ISN'T SO
ONE WILD NIGHT
BORN TO BE MY BABY
IT'S MY LIFE
BED OF ROSES
TWO STORY TOWN
JUST OLDER
RUNAWAY
LAY YOUR HANDS ON ME
I'LL SLEEP WHEN I'M DEAD
BAD MEDICINE
WANTED DEAD OR ALIVE
I'LL BE THERE FOR YOU
NEXT 100 YEARS
SOMEDAY I'LL BE SATURDAY NIGHT
KEEP THE FAITH
THANK YOU FOR LOVING ME

LOST HIGHWAY UNPLUGGED
WHO SAYS YOU CAN'T GO HOME
LOST HIGHWAY
YOU GIVE LOVE A BAD NAME
LIVIN' ON A PRAYER
YOU WANT TO MAKE A MEMORY
HALLELUJAH
IT'S MY LIFE
TILL WE AIN'T STRANGERS ANYMORE
BED OF ROSES
WHOLE LOT OF LEAVING
ANY OTHER DAY
THE LAST NIGHT

THIS LEFT FEELS RIGHT (Includes 6 poker wins)
LOVE FOR SALE
YOU GIVE LOVE A BAD NAME
WANTED DEAD OR ALIVE
LIVIN' ON A PRAYER
IT'S MY LIFE
MISUNDERSTOOD
LAY YOUR HANDS ON ME
SOMEDAY I'LL BE SATURDAY NIGHT
LAST MAN STANDING
SYLVIA'S MOTHER
EVERYDAY
BAD MEDICINE
BED OF ROSES
BORN TO BE MY BABY
KEEP THE FAITH
JOEY
THIEF OF HEARTS
I'LL BE THERE FOR YOU
ALWAYS
BLOOD ON BLOOD
VIDEO JUKEBOX LIVE IN HYDE PARK LONDON 2003
LAY YOUR HANDS ON ME
RAISE YOUR HANDS
CAPTAIN CRASH AND THE BEAUTY QUEEN FROM MARS
BLOOD ON BLOOD
BOUNCE
EVERYDAY
DIRECTOR'S VIEWS (MULTI CAMS)
LOVE FOR SALE

I'LL BE THERE FOR YOU
LAY YOUR HANDS ON ME

LIVE AT MADISON SQUARE GARDEN
LOST HIGHWAY
BORN TO BE MY BABY
BLAZE OF GLORY
IT'S MY LIFE
KEEP THE FAITH
RAISE YOUR HANDS
LIVING IN SIN
CHAPEL OF LOVE
ALWAYS
WHOLE LOT OF LEAVING
IN THESE ARMS
WE GOT IT GOING ON
I'LL BE THERE FOR YOU
YOU WANT TO MAKE A MEMORY
BLOOD ON BLOOD
DRY COUNTY
HAVE A NICE DAY
WHO SAYS YOU CAN'T GO HOME
HALLELUJAH
WANTED DEAD OR ALIVE
LIVIN' ON A PRAYER
BAD MEDICINE
YOU GIVE LOVE A BAD NAME
RUNAWAY
BED OF ROSES

KEEP THE FAITH VIDEO
WITH A LITTLE HELP FROM MY FRIENDS
LOVE FOR SALE
LAY YOUR HANDS ON ME
BLAZE OF GLORY
LITTLE BIT OF SOUL
BROTHER LOUIE
BED OF ROSES
LIVIN' ON A PRAYER
FEVER
IT'S MY LIFE
WE GOTTA GET OUT OF THIS PLACE
WANTED DEAD OR ALIVE
I'LL SLEEP WHEN I'M DEAD

BAD MEDICINE
KEEP THE FAITH

SLIPPERY WHEN WET VIDEO
WILD IN THE STREETS
LIVIN' ON A PRAYER
YOU GIVE LOVE A BAD NAME
NEVER SAY GOODBYE
LIVIN' ON A PRAYER
WANTED DEAD OR ALIVE

ACCESS ALL AREAS VIDEO
THE MAJORITY OF INCOMPLETE SONGS
LAY YOUR HANDS ON ME
PURPLE RAIN
STICK TO YOUR GUNS
BAD MEDICINE
I GOT ME A WOMAN
WANTED DEAD OR ALIVE
99 IN THE SHADE
TOKYO ROAD
RUNAWAY
WILD IS THE WIND
TRAVELLING BAND
YOU GIVE LOVE A BAD NAME
SOCIAL DISEASE
RIDE COWBOY RIDE
HAPPY BIRTHDAY ALEC
LIVIN' ON A PRAYER
THE BOYS ARE BACK IN TOWN
GOIN' BACK
SHOOTING STAR
LOVE FOR SALE
WE'RE HAVING A PARTY
RAWHIDE
HOMEBOUND TRAIN
LAY YOUR HANDS ON ME
WILD IN THE STREETS
I'LL BE THERE FOR YOU
LAY YOUR HANDS ON ME
WANTED DEAD OR ALIVE
AMERICAN BAND
YOU KEEP ME HANGING ON
WILD THING

YOU GIVE LOVE A BAD NAME
BRIDGE OVER TROUBLED WATERS
LIVIN' ON A PRAYER
SUPER ROCK 84
SHE DON'T KNOW ME
BREAK OUT
GET READY
RUNAWAY

AN EVENING WITH BON JOVI
KEEP THE FAITH
BED OF ROSES
IN THESE ARMS
IF I WAS YOUR MOTHER
I'LL SLEEP WHEN I'M DEAD
I BELIEVE
I WISH EVERYDAY COULD BE LIKE CHRISTMAS
CAMA DE ROSA (BED OF ROSES, SPANISH VERSION)
BALLAD OF YOUTH
DYIN' AIN'T MUCH OF A LIVIN'
I'LL SLEEP WHEN I'M DEAD

CROSS ROAD VIDEO
LIVIN' ON A PRAYER
KEEP THE FAITH
WANTED DEAD OR ALIVE
LAY YOUR HANDS ON ME
YOU GIVE LOVE A BAD NAME
BED OF ROSES
BLAZE OF GLORY
IN THESE ARMS
BAD MEDICINE
I'LL BE THERE FOR YOU
DRY COUNTY
LIVIN' IN SIN
MIRACLE
I BELIEVE
I'LL SLEEP WHEN I'M DEAD
ALWAYS

THE BREAKOUT VIDEOS
IN AND OUT OF LOVE
ONLY LONELY
SILENT NIGHT

SHE DON'T KNOW ME
HARDEST PART OF THE NIGHT
RUNAWAY

NEW JERSEY VIDEO
BAD MEDICINE
BORN TO BE MY BABY
I'LL BE THERE FOR YOU
LAY YOUR HANDS ON ME
LIVIN' IN SIN
BLOOD ON BLOOD
BAD MEDICINE

FINAL COUNTDOWN LIVE TOKYO DOME 1989 – 1990
TOKYO ROAD
YOU GIVE LOVE A BAD NAME
BORN TO BE MY BABY
I'LL BE THERE FOR YOU
BLOOD ON BLOOD
LIVIN' ON A PRAYER

LIVE NEW YEARS EVE TOKYO JAPAN 1988 – 1989
LAY YOUR HANDS ON ME
I'D DIE FOR YOU
WILD IN THE STREETS
YOU GIVE LOVE A BAD NAME
TOKYO ROAD
BORN TO BE MY BABY
I'LL BE THERE FOR YOU
BLOOD ON BLOOD
LIVIN' ON A PRAYER
RIDE COWBOY RIDE
WANTED DEAD OR ALIVE
BAD MEDICINE
ALL OVER NOW

TOKYO ROAD LIVE IN JAPAN 1985
TOKYO ROAD
BREAKOUT
ONLY LONELY
SHE DON'T KNOW ME
SHOT THROUGH THE HEART
SILENT NIGHT
HARDEST PART OF THE NIGHT

IN AND OUT OF LOVE
RUNAWAY
BURNING FOR LOVE
GET READY

TV SHOWS IN JAPAN 1987
RUNAWAY
ONLY LONELY
LIVIN' ON A PRAYER
YOU GIVE LOVE A BAD NAME

MOSCOW MUSIC PEACE FESTIVAL 1989
LAY YOUR HANDS ON ME
WILD IN THE STREETS
BLOOD ON BLOOD
WANTED DEAD OR ALIVE
LIVIN' ON A PRAYER
HOUND DOG
ROCK AND ROLL

SUPER ROCK 84
GET READY
RUNAWAY

THESE DAYS THE VIDEOS 1996
THIS AIN'T A LOVE SONG
SOMETHING FOR THE PAIN
THESE DAYS
LIE TO ME
HEY GOD
DAMNED
HEY GOD
THIS AIN'T A LOVE SONG
THESE DAYS

DAYTONA SPEEDWAY 2006 & ACOUSTIC LIVE JAPAN 1994
DAYTONA SPEEDWAY 2006
IT'S MY LIFE
HAVE A NICE DAY
WHO SAYS YOU CAN'T GO HAME
JAPAN ACOUSTIC SET 22/04/1994
LIVIN' ON A PRAYER
JUST LIKE A WOMAN
BED OF ROSES

WANTED DEAD OR ALIVE

LIVE AT THE ROCK AM RING 1995
LIVIN' ON A PRAYER
YOU GIVE LOVE A BAD NAME
KEEP THE FAITH
THIS AIN'T A LOVE SONG
WANTED DEAD OR ALIVE
LAY YOUR HANDS ON ME

LIVE FROM WEMBLEY STADIUM 1995
LIVIN' ON A PRAYER
YOU GIVE LOVE A BAD NAME
WILD IN THE STREETS
KEEP THE FAITH
BLOOD ON BLOOD
ALWAYS
I'D DIE FOR YOU
BLAZE OF GLORY
RUNAWAY
DRY COUNTY
LAY YOUR HANDS ON ME
I'LL SLEEP WHEN I'M DEAD
PAPA WAS A ROLLING STONE
BAD MEDICINE
SHOUT
BED OF ROSES
HEY GOD
ROCKIN ALL OVER THE WORLD
WANTED DEAD OR ALIVE
SOMEDAY I'LL BE SATURDAY NIGHT
GOOD GUYS DON'T ALWAYS WEAR WHITE
THIS AIN'T A LOVE SONG

LIVE IN BUENOS AIRES ARGENTINA 1993
I BELIEVE
WILD IN THE STREETS
YOU GIVE LOVE A BAD NAME
BORN TO BE MY BABY
CAMA DE ROSA
KEEP THE FAITH
BLOOD MONEY
BLAZE OF GLORY
LAY YOUR HANDS ON ME

I'LL SLEEP WHEN I'M DEAD
HELP
WANTED DEAD OR ALIVE
IN THESE ARMS
LIVIN' ON A PRAYER
HAPPY BIRTHDAY TO ALEC

LIVE IN BUENOS AIRES ARGENTINA 1995
ROCKIN ALL OVER THE WORLD
HEY GOD
LIVIN' ON A PRAYER
YOU GIVE LOVE A BAD NAME
KEEP THE FAITH
THESE DAYS
I'LL BE THERE FOR YOU
SOMEDAY I'LL BE SATURDAY NIGHT
BLOOD ON BLOOD
SOMETHING FOR THE PAIN
DIAMOND RING
DAMNED
BLAZE OF GLORY
LAY YOUR HANDS ON ME
I'LL SLEEP WHEN I'M DEAD
BAD MEDICINE
SHOUT
ALWAYS
WANTED DEAD OR ALIVE
BORN TO BE MY BABY
THIS AIN'T A LOVE SONG
COMO YO NADIE TE HA ARMDO

LIVE IN BUFFALO NY 02/17/1993
I BELIEVE
WILD IN THE STREETS
YOU GIVE LOVE A BAD NAME
BORN TO BE MY BABY
CAN'T HELP FALLING IN LOVE
BED OF ROSES
KEEP THE FAITH
I'D DIE FOR YOU
BLOOD MONEY
BLAZE OF GLORY
LAY YOUR HANDS ON ME
I'LL SLEEP WHEN I'M DEAD

JUMPIN JACK FLASH
BLOOD ON BLOOD
BAD MEDICINE
SHOUT
WANTED DEAD OR ALIVE
WITH A LITTLE HELP FROM MY FRIENDS
LIVIN' ON A PRAYER
NEVER SAY GOODBYE

LIVE IN RIO DE JANIERO BRAZIL 1990
LAY YOUR HANDS ON ME
I'D DIE FOR YOU
WILD IN THE STREETS
YOU GIVE LOVE A BAD NAME
BORN TO BE MY BABY
KEYBOARD SOLO
LET IT ROCK
I'LL BE THERE FOR YOU
BLOOD ON BLOOD
LIVIN' ON A PRAYER
TOKYO ROAD
RUNAWAY
NEVER SAY GOODBYE
WANTED DEAD OR ALIVE
BAD MEDICINE

LIVE IN SANTIAGO DE CHILE 1990
LAY YOUR HANDS ON ME
I'D DIE FOR YOU
WILD IN THE STREETS
YOU GIVE LOVE A BAD NAME
FEVER
BORN TO BE MY BABY
LET IT ROCK
I'LL BE THERE FOR YOU
BLOOD ON BLOOD
LIVIN' ON A PRAYER

LIVE IN SAO PAULO BRAZIL 1995
THESE DAYS
I'LL BE THERE FOR YOU
ROCKIN' IN THE FREE WORLD
LIVIN' ON A PRAYER
YOU GIVE LOVE A BAD NAME

KEEP THE FAITH
SOMEDAY I'LL BE SATURDAY NIGHT
DIAMOND RING
DIAMOND RING
I'LL SLEEP WHEN I'M DEAD
BAD MEDICINE

LIVE IN SEOUL SOUTH KOREA OLYMPIC STADIUM 1995
DVD 1
YOU GIVE LOVE A BAD NAME
WILD IN THE STREETS
KEEP THE FAITH
I'D DIE FOR YOU
DIAMOND RING
BED OF ROSES
STRANGER IN THIS TOWN
BLAZE OF GLORY
DRY COUNTY
BLOOD ON BLOOD
LAY YOUR HANDS ON ME
DVD 2
I'LL SLEEP WHEN I'M DEAD
JUMPIN JACK FLASH
GLORY DAYS
BAD MEDICINE
SHOUT
WITH A LITTLE HELP FROM MY FRIENDS
ALWAYS
LIVIN' ON A PRAYER
GUITAR SOLO
WANTED DEAD OR ALIVE
SOMEDAY I'LL BE SATURDAY NIGHT

LIVE IN YOKOHAMA JAPAN 1996
DVD 1
INTRODUCTION
LAY YOUR HANDS ON ME
BAD MEDICINE
HEY GOD
YOU GIVE LOVE A BAD NAME
RUNAWAY
I'LL BE THERE FOR YOU
SOMETHING TO BELIEVE IN
BLOOD ON BLOOD

WANTED DEAD OR ALIVE
I'D DIE FOR YOU
IN THESE ARMS
SOMETHING FOR THE PAIN
SOMEDAY I'LL BE SATURDAY NIGHT
I'LL SLEEP WHEN I'M DEAD
BROWN SUGAR
KEEP THE FAITH
DVD 2
ALWAYS
BLAZE OF GLORY
THESE DAYS
MY GUITAR LIES BLEEDING IN MY ARMS
DIAMOND RING
DAMNED
LIVING IN SIN

LIVE JAKARTA INDONESIA 1995
WILD IN THE STREETS
YOU GIVE LOVE A BAD NAME
KEEP THE FAITH
BED OF ROSES
LAY YOUR HANDS ON ME
BAD MEDICINE
WITH A LITTLE HELP FROM MY FRIENDS
ALWAYS
LIVIN' ON A PRAYER
NEVER SAY GOODBYE
SOMEDAY I'LL BE SATURDAY NIGHT

RED BANK NEW JERSEY CHRISTMAS SHOW 1996
ALL I WANT IS EVERY THING
DAMNED
THESE DAYS
YOU GIVE LOVE A BAD NAME
I'LL BE THERE FOR YOU
SOMEDAY I'LL BE SATURDAY NIGHT
ROCKIN ALL OVER THE WORLD
KEEP THE FAITH
WANTED DEAD OR ALIVE
RUN RUN RUDOLPH
WHAT A WONDERFUL WORLD
THE CHANUKAH SONG
I'LL SLEEP WHEN I'M DEAD

BLOOD ON BLOOD

TARATATA PARIS FRANCE 22/03/1996
KEEP THE FAITH
I DON'T LIKE MONDAYS
SAVE THE LAST DANCE FOR ME
LIE TO ME
SOMETHING FOR THE PAIN
THESE DAYS

TOP OF THE POPS BBC
BAD MEDICINE
IT'S MY LIFE
I'LL SLEEP WHEN I'M DEAD
SAY IT ISN'T SO
WANTED DEAD OR ALIVE
ALWAYS
THANK YOU FOR LOVING ME
KEEP THE FAITH
YOU GIVE LOVE A BAD NAME
LIVIN' ON A PRAYER

CRUSH THE VIDEOS 2001
IT'S MY LIFE
SAY IT ISN'T SO
ONE WILD NIGHT
THANK YOU FOR LOVING ME
TWO STORY TOWN
JUST OLDER
THANK YOU FOR LOVING ME
ONE WILD NIGHT

LIVE AT THE ZEPP CLUB TOKYO JAPAN 2002
UNDIVIDED
LIVIN' ON A PRAYER
YOU GIVE LOVE A BAD NAME
EVERYDAY
BORN TO BE MY BABY
JUST OLDER
BOUNCE
THE DISTANCE
WANTED DEAD OR ALIVE
KEEP THE FAITH
I'LL SLEEP WHEN I'M DEAD

BAD MEDICINE
BLOOD ON BLOOD
IT'S MY LIFE
EVERYDAY
UNDIVIDED
MISUNDERSTOOD
WANTED DEAD OR ALIVE
EVERYDAY
EVERYDAY

LIVE TIMES SQUARE 2002
IT'S MY LIFE
LIVIN' ON A PRAYER
YOU GIVE LOVE A BAD NAME
BORN TO BE MY BABY
JUST OLDER
EVERYDAY
UNDIVIDED
BOUNCE
I'LL SLEEP WHEN I'M DEAD
BAD MEDICINE
SHOUT
AMERICA THE BEAUTIFUL

ONE LAST WILD NIGHT NEW JERSEY 2001
ONE WILD NIGHT
RAISE YOUR HANDS
YOU GIVE LOVE A BAD NAME
BORN TO BE MY BABY
LIVIN' ON A PRAYER
BED OF ROSES
BLAZE OF GLORY
JUST OLDER
WILD IN THE STREETS
IT'S MY LIFE
KEEP THE FAITH
WANTED DEAD OR ALIVE
LAY YOUR HANDS ON ME
BAD MEDICINE
SHOUT

BOUNCE THE VIDEOS 2003
UNDIVIDED
EVERYDAY

THE DISTANCE
JOEY
MISUNDERSTOOD
ALL ABOUT LOVIN' YOU
HOOK ME UP
RIGHT SIDE OF WRONG
LOVE ME BACK TO LIFE
YOU HAD ME FROM HELLO
BOUNCE
OPEN ALL NIGHT

ONE WILD MELBOURNE NIGHT 2001
INTRO
ONE WILD NIGHT
YOU GIVE LOVE A BAD NAME
CAPTAIN CRASH AND THE BEAUTY QUEEN FROM MARS
IT'S MY LIFE
LIVIN' ON A PRAYER
JUST OLDER
BORN TO BE MY BABY
LAY YOUR HANDS ON ME
I'LL SLEEP WHEN I'M DEAD
BAD MEDICINE
SHOUT
WANTED DEAD OR ALIVE
KEEP THE FAITH
GOOD TIMES
RIDE THE NIGHT AWAY
TEQUILA
TWIST AND SHOUT

VH1 STORYTELLERS 2001
YOU GIVE LOVE A BAD NAME
IT'S MY LIFE
BED OF ROSES
LIVIN' ON A PRAYER
WANTED DEAD OR ALIVE
JUST OLDER
BAD MEDICINE
MISUNDERSTOOD

TV SPECIAL IN GERMANY 2002 & 2003
MISUNDERSTOOD
ALL ABOUT LOVIN'YOU

MISUNDERSTOOD
SOMEDAY I'LL BE SATURDAY NIGHT
EVERYDAY
WANTED DEAD OR ALIVE
LIVIN' ON A PRAYER

HAVE A NICE DAY TOUR LIVE IN JAPAN 2005
HAVE A NICE DAY
WELCOME TO WHEREVER YOU ARE
WHO SAYS YOU CAN'T GO HOME
HAVE A NICE DAY
HAVE A NICE DAY

BOUNCE PROMO TOUR 2003
HOOK ME UP
THE DISTANCE
MISUNDERSTOOD
BOUNCE
EVERYDAY
EVERYDAY
MISUNDERSTOOD
ALL ABOUT LOVIN'YOU

LIVE BORGATA CASINO 2004
WHY AREN'T YOU DEAD
YOU GIVE LOVE A BAD NAME
THE RADIO SAVED MY LIFE TONIGHT
BORN TO BE MY BABY
OPEN ALL NIGHT
EVERYDAY
MISS FOURTH OF JULY
IT'S MY LIFE
I'LL BE THERE FOR YOU
LOVE AIN'T NOTHING BUT A FOUR LETTER WORD
WANTED DEAD OR ALIVE
ONLY IN MY DREAMS
I GET A RUSH
I'LL SLEEP WHEN I'M DEAD
BAD MEDICINE
SHOUT
THESE ARMS ARE OPEN ALL NIGHT
GARAGELAND
LIVIN' ON A PRAYER

LIVE HAMMERSTEIN BALLROOM NY 2003
IT'S MY LIFE
EVERYDAY
YOU GIVE LOVE A BAD NAME
BOUNCE
BORN TO BE MY BABY
JUST OLDER
MISUNDERSTOOD
WANTED DEAD OR ALIVE
HOOK ME UP

CMT CROSS ROADS 2005
LIVIN' ON A PRAYER
SOMETHING MORE
IT'S MY LIFE
BABY GIRL
HAVE A NICE DAY
WANTED DEAD OR ALIVE
MAKE ME BELIEVE
WHO SAYS YOU CAN'T GO HOME

COMCAST SPECIAL COLUMBUS OHIO 2005
YOU GIVE LOVE A BAD NAME
COMPLICATED
BORN TO BE MY BABY
STORY OF MY LIFE
RUNAWAY
WHO SAYS YOU CAN'T GO HOME
RADIO SAVED MY LIFE TONIGHT
HAVE A NICE DAY

LIVE IN AMSTERDAM 2005
LAST MAN STANDING
YOU GIVE LOVE A BAD NAME
LIVIN' ON A PRAYER
BORN TO BE MY BABY
HAVE A NICE DAY
IT'S MY LIFE
THE RADIO SAVED MY LIFE TONIGHT
SOMEDAY I'LL BE SATURDAY NIGHT
WANTED DEAD OR ALIVE
WHO SAYS YOU CAN'T GO HOME
I'LL SLEEP WHEN I'M DEAD
RAISE YOUR HANDS

KEEP THE FAITH
BAD MEDICINE
HAVE A NICE DAY

LIVE IN GILLETE STADIUM FOXBORO 2006
LAST MAN STANDING
YOU GIVE LOVE A BAD NAME
BOUNCE
I'LL SLEEP WHEN I'M DEAD
RADIO SAVED MY LIFE TONIGHT
IN THESE ARMS
JUST OLDER
BAD MEDICINE
SHOUT
BAD MEDICINE
WANTED DEAD OR ALIVE
BLOOD ON BLOOD

LIVE IN NOKIA THEATRE NEW YORK 2005 + TV SHOW
LAST MAN STANDING
YOU GIVE LOVE A BAD NAME
LIVIN' ON A PRAYER
BORN TO BE MY BABY
HAVE A NICE DAY
IT'S MY LIFE
THE RADIO SAVED MY LIFE TONIGHT
SOMEDAY I'LL BE SATURDAY NIGHT
WANTED DEAD OR ALIVE
WHO SAYS YOU CAN'T GO HOME
I'LL SLEEP WHEN I'M DEAD
RAISE YOUR HANDS
KEEP THE FAITH
TREAT HER RIGHT
BAD MEDICINE

ACOUSTIC NIGHT IN MEXICO CITY 1997
LOVE FOR SALE
EVERY WORD WAS A PIECE OF MY HEART
PRAYER 94
MIDNIGHT IN CHELSEA
JANIE, DON'T TAKE YOUR LOVE TO TOWN
BED OF ROSES
UGLY
KNOCKIN' ON HEAVENS DOOR

DESTINATION ANYWHERE
BLOOD ON BLOOD
WANTED DEAD OR ALIVE

LIVE AT THE ROCK IN RIO LISBON PORTUGAL 05/31/2008
BORN TO BE MY BABY
YOU GIVE LOVE A BAD NAME
RAISE YOUR HANDS
RUNAWAY
I'LL SLEEP WHEN I'M DEAD
START ME UP
WHOLE LOT OF LEAVING
IN THESE ARMS
ALWAYS
WE GOT IT GOING ON
IT'S MY LIFE
KEEP THE FAITH
I'LL BE THERE FOR YOU
BLAZE OF GLORY
WHO SAYS YOU CAN'T GO HOME
HAVE A NICE DAY
BAD MEDICINE
SHOUT
LIVIN' ON A PRAYER
SOMEDAY I'LL BE SATURDAY NIGHT
WANTED DEAD OR ALIVE

TV SHOW LIVE EARTH, TODAY SHOW & THE VIEW 2007
LIVE EARTH 2007
LOST HIGHWAY
IT'S MY LIFE
WANTED DEAD OR ALIVE
WHO SAYS YOU CAN'T GO HOME
LIVIN' ON A PRAYER
TODAY SHOW NBC 2007
WHO SAYS YOU CAN'T GO HOME
YOU WANT TO MAKE A MEMORY
LOST HIGHWAY
WHOLE LOT OF LEAVING
THE VIEW 2007
YOU WANT TO MAKE A MEMORY
WHO SAYS YOU CAN'T GO HOME

LIVE FROM TOKYO DOME JAPAN 01/14/2008
LOST HIGHWAY
YOU GIVE LOVE A BAD NAME
RAISE YOUR HANDS
RUNAWAY
THE RADIO SAVED MY LIFE TONIGHT
STORY OF MY LIFE
IN THESE ARMS
I'D DIE FOR YOU
(YOU WANT TO) MAKE A MEMORY
WHOLE LOT OF LEAVING
BORN TO BE MY BABY
ANY OTHER DAY
WE GOT IT GOING ON
IT'S MY LIFE
BAD MEDICINE
SHOUT
THESE DAYS
SOMEDAY I'LL BE SATURDAY NIGHT
KEEP THE FAITH
I'LL SLEEP WHEN I'M DEAD
JUMPIN JACK FLASH
DANCING IN THE STREETS
WHO SAYS YOU CAN'T GO HOME
LIVIN' ON A PRAYER
HAVE A NICE DAY
WANTED DEAD OR ALIVE
I LOVE THIS TOWN
CAPTAIN CRASH AND THE BEAUTY QUEEN FROM MARS

AOL ACOUSTIC SESSIONS NRG STUDIOS BURBANK CA 2002
AOL ACOUSTIC SESSIONS BURBANK, CA 2002
LOVE FOR SALE
SOMEDAY I'LL BE SATURDAY NIGHT
JOEY
MISUNDERSTOOD
DIAMOND RING
BLOOD ON BLOOD
ACOUSTIC LIVE YOKOHAMA ARENA 2003
IN THESE ARMS
HEROES
RIGHT SIDE OF WRONG (MONTAGE)

LIVE ACOUSTIC & ELECTRIC SHOW KIEL GERMANY 2003
ACOUSTIC SHOW
HAVE A LITTLE FAITH IN ME
LOVE FOR SALE
LIVIN' ON A PRAYER
WANTED DEAD OR ALIVE
SOMEDAY I'LL BE SATURDAY NIGHT
SOMETHING TO BELIEVE IN
BED OF ROSES
EVERYDAY
DIAMOND RING
BLOOD ON BLOOD
THE DISTANCE
FEVER
LIVING IN SIN
HEROES
ELECTRIC SHOW
JOEY
MISUNDERSTOOD
IN THESE ARMS
RUNAWAY
YOU GIVE LOVE A BAD NAME
IT'S MY LIFE
BORN TO BE MY BABY
I'LL SLEEP WHEN I'M DEAD
ROCKIN ALL OVER THE WORLD
RAISE YOUR HANDS
THESE DAYS
NEVER SAY GOODBYE

LIVE THE FORUM LONDON 1997
NOT FADE AWAY
EVERY WORD WAS A PIECE OF MY HEART
QUEEN OF NEW ORLEANS
MIDNIGHT IN CHELSEA
DESTINATION ANYWHERE
LIVIN' ON A PRAYER
NAKED
JAILBREAK
I'LL SLEEP WHEN I'M DEAD

BIBLIOGRAPHY

The song I Talk To Jesus I found on the net.
http://artists.letssingit.com/bon-jovi-lyrics-i-talk to jesus-nxsj84f

The Band pictures, David Bryan and Alec John Such's pictures come
from the following sites:
Big Robbo-MFA.Admin/Deity (2010) Mamas Fallen Angels pages 8,
40, 50,
50, Cover page 67
http://www.mamasfallenangels.com/group/bonjovi/forum/topics/66004
6:Topic45514
http://persimusic.files.wordpress.com/2009/06/bon-jovi.jpg
http://www.men-access.com/wp-content/uploads/2009/04/bon-jovi-
25th-anniversary.jpg
http://media.photobucket.com/image/bon%20jovi%20band/jonnie_200
7/BON%20JOVI%20BAND/86f9.jpg?o=220

Jon Bon Jovi's picture site: Big Robbo-MFA.Admin/Deity (2010)
Mamas Fallen Angels page 2
http://www.mamasfallenangels.com/group/bonjovi/forum/topics/66004
6:Topic45514

Richie Sambora's picture site: http:exc.images-
amazon.com/images/1LOevXEfTL._SL600_.jpg

Tico Torres's picture site:
http://people.famouswhy.com/tico_torres/tico_torres_picture1_13.jpg

Hugh McDonald's picture site:
http://www.zemaitis.nct/images/players/hugh-mcdonald-bon-jovi.jpg

ABOUT THE AUTHOR

I was 59 years old; a mother of three very special and supportive children and a grandmother of three wonderful grandsons (I now have five grand-children) when I started writing this first book whilst watching a Bon Jovi concert DVD. (I am an avid fan, if you can call me that; crazy is more like it.)

As the concert progressed, I started to put the song titles of the songs they were playing in sentences. From there I began writing short stories of about one page using the other band members works. As I like a challenge, I decided to try bigger stories using more song titles and the biggest challenge was this book.

I write from the heart and I really enjoyed writing the book so I wrote another, using different artists and the books kept coming to me and I kept writing them.(with a little help from above.)

Because I use different artist/artists song titles I have to be very careful with Copyright so a lot of legal requirements have to be taken into consideration before publishing the books. I also needed a name that would connect my books to each other; so the "Song Title Series" books began.

All my books are short stories; however it depends on how many song titles there are to be used, as to the length of the book. Some artists didn't have enough song titles on their own so I combined them with a few other artists. Other artists had that many song titles that I could have written a novel; but it would have ended up being boring.

Challenges I like, so writing books with various artists are a lot of fun and careful thinking.

Why should I have all the fun writing the books and not be able to share them with everyone; so I have converted them into large print books and E-books so that you can share my fun as well.

Hopefully in the not too distant future; the books will also be available as audio books so that no-one will miss out on my fun and enjoyment of writing these unique books. I hope that you will enjoy reading them.

My web site www.songtitleseries.com is the place to visit for updates of new books and to purchase other titles in all formats.

OTHER BOOKS IN THE SONG TITLE SERIES

Bon Jovi – Wanted Dead Or Alive
Green Day
AC/DC
Beach Boys
Slim Dusty
Country Women
Five Country Men
Six Crooners
Three Crooners
ABBA
The Rat Pack
Elton John
Classic 50s & 60s Rock 'N' Roll

TESTIMONIALS

Joan Maguire Books are very nice, I enjoy reading them so much, they are hard to put down!! Especially when she does one about Bonjovi and their songs!!!
If I can say, it is worth every penny, when you buy one!!! The Books make nice presents, for a person whom loves to read!!! I can guarantee that you will LOVE these books, because I do!!!!!!!!!
Dawn from Newark, Delaware in the United States of America

I am Susie and would like to tell you guys, how much I am enjoying Joan Maguire's Books!! They are very enjoyable, and they are something that you do not ever want to put down!! I really enjoy these books; I can't wait until the next one that she puts out!!!!!!! I say go to your local book store, today and get one, you will not be disappointed!!!!!
Sue-from the United States of America

The song titles series are books that were intriguing and were hard to believe that these short stories were written within the incorporated song titles of the artists that are mentioned in the titles. I loved what I have read so far and think that anyone with an imagination and love of music as the author you will surely enjoy reading these.
L.K. Brisbane Australia.

After reading through your range of books I felt I must compliment you Joan on the imaginative and entertaining way in which you presented each group and the Musicians in those groups. The way the stories were constructed is a credit to your work ethic. These must have taken considerable time to piece together and it is obviously a work of love for you.
I wish you all the success you truly deserve and look forward to seeing you next time you visit Tamworth.
Peter Harkins
Managing Director Cheapa Music
Country Music Capital Tamworth

www.ingramcontent.com/pod-product-compliance
Lightning Source LLC
Chambersburg PA
CBHW062000040426
42447CB00010B/1836